"Christians tend to shun the boo[k] for ethical instruction and spiritua[l] shows, with the aid of modern to miss some of the most relevant messages of Scripture. Reading these apparently unpromising texts with Beldman, you will be instructed and challenged. In short, this is a most worthwhile study of a valuable part of the Bible."

—Gordon J. Wenham, tutor in Old Testament, Trinity College (Bristol, England); author, *Exploring the Old Testament*

"The 'church' in our times is in desperate need of a deep plunge into the book of Judges. I know no one better to guide that plunge than David Beldman. Prior to our church preaching through the book of Judges, David guided our leaders through *Deserting the King*. It was stunning, formative, and sharpening. I highly encourage all to engage Judges through this book."

—Tyler Johnson, lead pastor, Redemption Church (Arizona)

"In this excellent survey, David Beldman does three things. He sets the book of Judges meaningfully within the overarching creational and redemptive narrative of the whole Bible; he clarifies and illuminates the structure of the book and the intrinsic (but easily overlooked) message that structure carries; and he offers penetrating reflections on the relevance of the book to contemporary cultures. To do all this in such a simply-written and easy-to-read short volume, and to do it for one of the more challenging and neglected books in the Bible, is a most commendable achievement. Church and student groups, preachers and teachers, will all find this book opens their eyes and feeds their faith."

—Christopher J.H. Wright, international ministries director, Langham Partnership

DESERTING THE KING

THE BOOK OF JUDGES

**Other titles in
the Transformative Word series:**

Glimpsing the Mystery: The Book of Daniel
by Barbara M. Leung Lai

God Behind the Scenes: The Book of Esther
by Wayne K. Barkhuizen

When You Want to Yell at God: The Book of Job
by Craig G. Bartholomew

Faith Amid the Ruins: The Book of Habakkuk
by Heath A. Thomas

Revealing the Heart of Prayer: The Gospel of Luke
by Craig G. Bartholomew

Together for the World: The Book of Acts
by Michael R. Wagenman

Cutting Ties with Darkness: 2 Corinthians
by John D. Barry

Between the Cross and the Throne: The Book of Revelation
by Matthew Y. Emerson

DESERTING THE KING

THE BOOK OF JUDGES

TRANSFORMATIVE WORD

DAVID J. H. BELDMAN

Edited by Craig G. Bartholomew

LEXHAM PRESS

Deserting the King: The Book of Judges
Transformative Word

Copyright 2017 David J. H. Beldman

Lexham Press, 1313 Commercial St., Bellingham, WA 98225
LexhamPress.com

Print ISBN 9781577997764
Digital ISBN 9781577997771

Series Editor: Craig G. Bartholomew
Lexham Editorial: Sarah Awa, Abby Salinger, Lynnea Smoyer,
            Abigail Stocker, Elizabeth Vince
Cover Design: Quincy Rouse
Typesetting: ProjectLuz.com

CONTENTS

"God is dead! God remains dead! And we have killed him! How can we console ourselves, the murderers of all murderers! The holiest and mightiest thing the world has ever possessed has bled to death under our knives: who will wipe this blood from us? With what water could we clean ourselves? What festivals of atonement, what holy games will we have to invent for ourselves? Is the magnitude of this deed not too great for us? Do we not ourselves have to become gods merely to appear worthy of it? There was never a greater deed—and whoever is born after us will on account of this deed belong to a higher history than all history up to now! ... What then are these churches now if not the tombs and sepulchres of God?"

—Nietzsche's Madman[1]

INTRODUCTION

Imagine that a friend comes to you. Her marriage of ten years has disintegrated, and she doesn't know what to do. She first noticed little warning signs about two years into the marriage. It was the way he looked at other women. He didn't know that she noticed, and she initially tried to ignore it. Eventually, she confronted her husband—and he didn't deny it. He apologized and promised to change, and things were better for a while. A number of years later, the woman noticed her husband flirting with a long-time friend at a birthday party. When she confronted him, he attributed his poor behavior to the multiple drinks he had consumed. Again, he apologized, and things went well for a while. In the last year, the husband's business consistently kept him busy, and he spent more time at the office and on short trips away from home. A few weeks ago, the woman found some texts on her husband's phone from one of his female employees. It was undeniable: Her husband was having an affair. The woman was deeply hurt and shocked. When she confronted her husband, he admitted that he was having an affair and confessed that he had been engaging in inappropriate behavior with other women throughout their entire marriage. This pattern of promiscuity had begun before their wedding, and although he had hoped that getting married would provide a fresh start, the old pattern soon emerged. The wife was devastated; she felt her marriage had been a sham from the beginning—that the vows she and her husband had made on their wedding day meant nothing.

This is the story that plays out on the pages of the book of Judges. Yahweh is like the faithful spouse, Israel is like the unfaithful husband, the Sinai covenant is like the marriage vows, and Israel's persistent service to the gods of the Canaanites is like the husband's painful betrayals of the marriage contract. Although we may get the sense that God's people gradually slide into unfaithfulness, by the end of Judges we realize that their infidelity is deeply rooted early in their relationship with Yahweh. Did the Sinai covenant and Israel's repeated assent to it have any meaning at all?

The book of Judges, which recounts a particular period in the life of God's people, is by no means glamorous. It shows the tragic situation of a persistently and repeatedly unfaithful people. Judges portrays a chapter in history when God's people, Israel, were maturing from an association of twelve tribes into a fully formed nation. But rather than living up to their calling as a holy nation and a kingdom of priests (Exod 19:6), the Israelites became like the surrounding nations in their character and conduct. The consequences for themselves and the nations were drastic.

The basic message of Judges is a divine summons for God's people to remember who they are and what King Yahweh has done for them. On that basis, they are to live out their calling as Yahweh's representatives on earth for the blessing of the nations. This message resounds through the centuries, and it continues to summon followers of Jesus like you and me to live out our calling amidst the challenges of the 21st century.

> The basic message of Judges is a divine summons for God's people to remember who they are and what King Yahweh has done for them.

Yet it can be easy to overlook this central message because Judges is such a complex and puzzling book. The book's puzzling nature is reflected at times by riddles within the stories themselves. For instance, at his wedding reception, Samson presented this riddle to his guests:

> Out of the eater came something to eat.
> Out of the strong came something sweet.
> (Judg 14:14)

Readers of Judges know that the inspiration behind Samson's riddle is the carcass of the lion that Samson killed, which had become home to a colony of honeybees (14:5–9). But if the story did not provide that information, we would be as stumped by the riddle as Samson's wedding guests were. This puzzle would seem impossible to solve.

Although the book of Judges contains some of the most memorable stories of the Bible—stories of bloodshed, intrigue, and heroism—it also presents readers with perplexing riddles that, like Samson's riddle, seem impossible to solve. Its complex and sometimes bizarre situations, characters, and behavior may at points cause us to wonder how this book could possibly prompt us to say, "This is the Word of the Lord; thanks be to God." Perhaps the most fundamental puzzle facing modern readers of Judges is: How do we attune our ears so that we might hear God speaking to us today through the book of Judges? While there are some puzzles in the book that we may never solve, Judges does provide us with unmistakable clues for understanding this perplexing—yet vital—part of the Bible.

Think of this book as a map to help you gain your bearings in the book of Judges. Maps are most helpful in places that are unfamiliar to us, but they can also help us find new areas to explore in familiar places. Most important, a map should never be an end in itself. It should always drive us back to the places it represents—to explore the riches of the terrain itself. I hope that, like a good map, this book helps you make your way through the sometimes-disorienting terrain of Judges and prompts you to return again and again to the biblical text itself.

Before we go further, it will be helpful to explore two important questions: (1) What is Judges (the book of the Bible), and (2) who are the judges (the individual leaders who appear in the book)?

Judges: The Book

Judges appears among the Old Testament books that come after the Pentateuch (Genesis–Deuteronomy) and before the poetic books (Job–Song of Songs). This section (which includes the books of Joshua, Judges, Ruth, 1–2 Samuel, 1–2 Kings, 1–2 Chronicles, Ezra, Nehemiah, and Esther) is commonly referred to as the historical books—not because the other books are not

OUTLINE

historical but because these books offer an account of Israel's history from the conquest of the land until the time following the return from exile. Judges covers the period after the conquest of Canaan (in Joshua) and before the rise of monarchy in Israel (1–2 Samuel). It accounts for the time in Israel's history when the Israelites settled in the promised land. This period is often called the "settlement period," though sometimes it is referred to as the "period of the judges" because during this time the Israelites were governed by judges. Judges is by no means exhaustive in its treatment of this period; it doesn't relate all of the events of the settlement period. However, it does give a general overview of Israel's history during this time. The book is selective in its content, but the events that do appear highlight what is essential about this period.

We should bear in mind that history writing in general is never a mere chronicle of one event after another. Historians carefully research, select, arrange, and craft their narrative of the events of history into something meaningful and coherent. This is also true of the historical accounts we find in the Bible. John testifies to this reality near the end of his Gospel. In John 21:25, he says that the whole world would not be able to contain all the volumes he could have written about the life and times of Jesus, and in John 20:30–31 he notes, "Jesus did many other signs in the presence of the disciples, which are not written in this book; but these are written so that you may believe that Jesus is the Christ, the Son of God, and that by believing you may have life in his name." This is John's purpose for writing his Gospel—namely, to move people to believe in the Messiah and find life in him. John's purpose profoundly influences the way he tells the story, including how he structures his account (seven signs, seven "I am" sayings), what he includes that the other Gospels do not (the water-into-wine miracle, the raising of Lazarus), and what he leaves out of his account (Jesus' baptism, temptation, and transfiguration). John's unique way of telling Jesus' story stems from his motivation to illuminate

Jesus' true identity for a generation of Christians in the latter half of the first century.

Unfortunately, Judges does not provide a clear purpose statement like John's Gospel does—which may be another one of the book's puzzles. However, the underlying composition principle is the same: Many events in the settlement period do not appear in Judges, and the things that do appear are included for a purpose. As we will see in detail in later chapters of this book, the author of Judges thoughtfully and carefully composed the book so as to convey a message. Perhaps the messages of Judges and John are not so different; Judges is an urgent plea for God's people to believe in Yahweh and find life in him.

> The message of the author of Judges to his audience resounds through the centuries so that it is the message of the living God for his people today.

Like in the Gospel of John, the message of Judges is mediated through the text of Judges. In a mysterious way, God, through the Holy Spirit, has worked through the means and motivations of human authors to produce holy Scripture. The words of the prophets and apostles in all their humanness become the word of God. The message of the author of Judges to his audience resounds through the centuries so that it is the message of the living God for his people today. By attending closely to the details and motivations of the human author, we put ourselves in the best position to hear God addressing us through Judges today.

We should regard all Old Testament historical narrative as history with a purpose. On this point, we can learn from Jewish tradition, which, since ancient times, has designated Judges among the Former Prophets.[1] Understanding Judges as prophetic literature is beneficial for a number for reasons. First, this view recognizes that Judges is God's word, which was delivered to a particular people for a specific purpose. In other words, the purpose of the book is not merely historical but theological. Second, it helps us recognize that historical events, when viewed through the proper lens, reveal God and his purposes. These events are valuable in that they disclose the character of God, the reality of the world he created, and his intentions for humanity in the world. As this is the case, Judges is most certainly prophetic. Finally, when we hear the message of Judges as addressed to its original audience, that message will echo through the ages so that it addresses us, too. The words of Judges are alive and active, speaking prophetically into our 21st-century contexts.

> The words of Judges are alive and active, speaking prophetically into our 21st-century contexts.

Judges: The People

The title of the book, "Judges," is a nod to the central characters of the book. We will distinguish between the major judges (e.g., Othniel, Ehud, Deborah, Gideon, Jephthah, and Samson) and the minor judges (e.g., Shamgar, Tola, Jair, Ibzan, Elon, and Abdon). The latter are minor only because Judges provides very limited information about them—sometimes only a verse or two. The accounts of the major judges, on the other hand, are more detailed and extensive.

The term "judges" may be a misleading title for these leaders, and it is thus perhaps not the best designation for the book. In ancient Israel, the office of judge did exist (see Exod 18:13–27; Deut 16:18–20). The judge's role was to arbitrate between disputes and, in particular cases, to make Yahweh's will and statutes known. The central figures in the book of Judges did apparently hold these offices. The Hebrew verb for "to judge" is applied in the book to four of the major judges (Othniel, Deborah, Jephthah, and Samson) and to five of the six minor judges (Shamgar being the exception), each of whom is said to have "judged" Israel. However, in only one case (that of Deborah) is anyone actually engaged in an activity related to the office of judge (see Judg 4:5), and Yahweh is the only one in the whole book to whom the title "judge" is specifically applied (11:27). The activity of judging probably took place after these individuals had brought about peace in the land by delivering the Israelites from their enemies.

Although these leaders did at some point engage in the activity of judging, their significance in the book of Judges is in their role as *deliverers*. In the one place in the book where the word applies to the judges collectively (2:16–19), the text immediately qualifies the significant function that they played: "Then Yahweh raised up judges, *who saved them* out of the hand of those who plundered them" (2:16, emphasis added). For all the faults of these leaders, Yahweh used them to deliver his people. This book will refer to these leaders as "judges" and as "deliverers" interchangeably.

Israel's God as the True Judge and the True King

Each narrative in Judges reveals more about the character of Israel's God and savior. While at times these characterizations are front and center, at other times they are barely discernible, though no less present. Yahweh is characterized in the book as both divine judge and king.[2] In Judges we may tend to focus on God's anger, his judgment, or his punishment, but we should not miss the book's portrayal of two other essential characteristics of God: his grace and longsuffering nature. Tough love does exist in Judges, but so does tender love. God patiently directs Israel's history so as to motivate them out of their rebellion; he hears their cry for help and responds with a savior; he desires prosperity for his people—and through his people for the whole world—and will carefully work through their choices and actions to bring that shalom to its fulfillment. This is the same God we have come to know in Jesus, who accomplished the kingdom of peace with his perfect life, sacrificial death, and miraculous resurrection.

> Judges may be a puzzling book, but it provides today's readers with essential truths about the God we serve.

Judges may be a puzzling book, but it provides today's readers with essential truths about the God we serve, about the human condition, and about our place and calling in the world. The ancient teachings in Judges are actually quite contemporary when we have the ears to hear them.

SUGGESTED READING

- ☐ Read the whole of Judges, in one sitting if possible.
- ☐ Read Judges 2:1–3:6 carefully.

Reflection

What stood out to you when you read through Judges? Did anything surprise you or confuse you? Jot those things down and return to them as you read this study.

_____

_____

_____

Is considering Judges as a prophetic book a new concept to you? How does reading Judges as a prophetic book affect how you approach or understand the book?

_____

_____

_____

Do you agree that God's purposes for his people in the world as they are portrayed in Judges are the same for his people and the world today? Why or why not?

_____

_____

_____

JUDGES IN THE CONTEXT OF THE GRAND STORY

The book of Judges is part of a larger story, a grand narrative that begins in Genesis 1 and ends in Revelation 22. The Bible is the comprehensive story of all things from Eden to the new Jerusalem, from God's creation of the heavens and the earth to the new heavens and the new earth. To hear and understand the message of Judges, it is crucial to understand its place in this grand narrative.

Considering the immediate surroundings of Judges, we notice that Judges follows on the heels of Joshua and precedes Ruth and the books of Samuel. The book of Ruth is set sometime in the period of the judges, as the opening line indicates: "In the days when the judges ruled" (Ruth 1:1). But the purposes of these two books from this period in Israel's history are quite different. Whereas the focus of Ruth is narrow (telling the story of Naomi, Ruth, and Boaz and concluding with the family line of David), the focus of Judges is much broader. Judges by no means covers all the events that took place during the period of the judges, but it does aim to fill in the historical gap between the period of the conquest (recounted in Joshua) and the rise of the united monarchy in Israel (told in the books of Samuel). So Judges gives us a window into the period in Israel's history after the tribes had made their home in the promised land but before the rise of kingship under Saul and then David.

God's Promises Given; Israel's Calling Established

If we trace the biblical narrative up to the period of Judges, we see that an important foundation of Israel's story is recounted early on. In Genesis 12, Yahweh calls Abraham to leave everything that would have provided him with safety, security, and identity (including land, society, and family) to go to an undisclosed location. God calls Abraham but also promises him specific blessings:

> Go from your country and your people
> and your father's house to the land
> that I will show you.
> And I will make of you a great nation,
> And I will bless you,
> And make your name great,
> And be a blessing.
> And I will bless those who bless you,
> And those who dishonor you I will
> curse,
> And in you all peoples on the earth
> shall be blessed. (Gen 12:1–3,
> author's translation)

David Clines summarizes the promises to the patriarchs as consisting of (1) posterity, (2) divine-human
relationship, and (3) land. In other words, Abraham
and his descendants would be a great and numerous
nation (posterity); they would have a relationship of
blessing with God and each other (and the nations);
and they would have a home—a land to call their
own in which they would live out God's intention for
the world.

God's calling of Abraham, however, is not the
beginning of the story either; we can trace its roots
even further back to Genesis 1-11. The opening chapters of Genesis illustrate for us the establishment of
the Creator-King's realm and subjects. God creates a
good, harmonious, and vibrant world, and he creates
humans in his image and tasks them to cultivate and
take care of his kingdom. But the first humans are
not content to be like God; they determine to be gods.
They rebel against their king and cast the world
into chaos.

Genesis 4-11 recounts the unleashing of sin
and rebellion into the world and God's response to
it—a response of both judgment and mercy. The harmonious relationships between humanity and God,
between the humans themselves, and between the
humans and creation seem irrevocably broken.
But God did not annihilate the world he had made;
his intentions for a world of blessing remain. God's
promises to Abraham—to make him and his descendants into a great nation, to establish a relationship
of blessing, and to provide him with land—were part
of a great plan to see God's good intention for the
world prevail. The last word would not be the curses

of Genesis 3:14–19 but the promised blessings of God's covenant relationship.

According to Clines, these promises are woven into the fabric of the Pentateuch (Genesis–Deuteronomy), but they are dominant in different parts. In fact, Clines rightly and helpfully describes the theme of the whole of the Pentateuch as "the partial fulfillment ... of the promises to ... the patriarchs" (to Abraham, Isaac, Jacob, and Jacob's sons).[1] God's promise to make Abraham into a great nation is dominant in the pages of Genesis so that when we turn the page into Exodus, the people of Israel are plentiful, overflowing the boundaries of their home in Egypt. God's promise to establish a relationship of blessing is forged especially when he brings the Israelites out of Egypt. At Mount Sinai, God gives Israel a new identity: They are to be a kingdom of priests and a holy nation (Exod 19:6). The Sinai covenant—what I refer to as the "Manifesto for a Holy Nation and a Priestly Kingdom"—spells out the nature of Yahweh's relationship with Israel and how the Israelites are to live out their new identity. Exodus and Leviticus recount the dimensions of this second aspect of the promises to Abraham. At the beginning of Numbers, the only element of promise yet to be fulfilled is the promise of the land.

Unfortunately, the Israelites rebel, and instead of entering the promised land right away, they take a long detour and wander in the desert for 40 years. By the end of Numbers, the people are back where they started and on the move toward the promised land. In Deuteronomy, the Israelites are on the Plains of Moab, looking out over the promised land. Deuteronomy also includes Moses' final instructions

THE MANIFESTO FOR A HOLY NATION AND A PRIESTLY KINGDOM

With the defeat of Pharaoh, Yahweh had demonstrated his rightful status as divine king and had rescued his people, Israel, from the grip of the oppressive usurper, Pharaoh. On the basis of this redemption, Yahweh gives his people a new identity—they are to be a holy nation and a kingdom of priests. To be holy meant that Israel would be set apart from the other nations, but they were set apart for a purpose. They were also to be a nation of priests, meaning they were to mediate Yahweh's blessing to the nations, confirming God's promise to Abraham that through his descendants all nations would be blessed.

Just how would God's people walk that fine line of being set apart from the nations (holy) for the sake of blessing the nations (priestly)? That's precisely what the stipulations of the Sinai covenant are for: to be their guide in living out Yahweh's good intentions for humanity and the world for the flourishing of the whole world. What Patrick Miller says of the Ten Commandments could be said about the whole of the Sinai covenant: "the Commandments are given for the creation and preservation of community, for producing a good neighborhood."[2] This is much more than a list of dos and don'ts; it is the means by which Israel would flourish and allow that flourishing to spill over to the surrounding nations. If Israel had followed the Manifesto for a Holy Nation and a Priestly Kingdom, we would expect a society to emerge that would have displayed Yahweh's intention for humanity and one that would have attracted the surrounding nations to enjoy the blessing of Yahweh too.

to the people before they cross over into the land. Numbers and Deuteronomy are very much about the promise of land, but by the end of Deuteronomy that promise is yet to be fulfilled.

In the book of Joshua, the people cross the Jordan River, and the period of the conquest begins. Yahweh goes before the 12 Israelite tribes and helps them take possession of the land. Joshua 13–21 recounts in painstaking detail the parceling out of the land and the territorial boundaries for each of the tribes. Why all of these repetitive details? The amount of space devoted to the parceling out of the land is an indication of its significance: The final promise God made to Abraham is now fulfilled.

An absolutely vital aspect of the promises to Abraham and the patriarchs—in fact, the ultimate aim of God's election of Abraham and his descendants—is that they would be a channel of blessing to the nations (the Gentiles). Notice that the goal of the promises to Abraham in Genesis 12:3 is that "in you all peoples on the earth shall be blessed." These words are repeated again and again as God makes and reaffirms the covenant with Abraham, Isaac, and Jacob (see Gen 18:17–19; 22:15–18; 26:3–4; 28:13–14). In Galatians 3:8, Paul even says that in these words to Abraham we have the essence of the gospel.

Moreover, Israel's vocation at Sinai to be a kingdom of priests and a holy nation is an unmistakable call to be a channel of blessing: By being a nation that is distinct and set apart from the pagan nations (a holy nation), the Israelites would mediate Yahweh's blessing to and intention for all nations (a kingdom of priests). They were to be a display nation—a society characterized by righteousness, justice, mercy for the oppressed, and shalom (the rich Old Testament concept of comprehensive flourishing)—so that the nations would be drawn to Israel to experience their blessed existence.

The book of Joshua ends with a covenant-renewal ceremony at which Joshua gives his final address to the people, urging them to remain faithful to Yahweh, their covenant king. He urges them to declare their allegiance: Will they serve the gods of the Canaanites, or will they be loyal to King Yahweh (Josh 24:15)? Three times the Israelite congregation eagerly expresses, "We will serve Yahweh!" (Josh 24:18, 21, 24). With these words ringing in our ears, we turn the page to the book of Judges. At this crucial point in history, we should be filled with a keen sense of anticipation and hope: All the promises that God made to Abraham and his descendants have been fulfilled, the people of Yahweh are committed to the service of Yahweh, and they are now poised to be that kingdom of priests and that holy nation who will flourish in their new home and mediate Yahweh's blessings to the Gentile nations.

God's Promises Fulfilled; Israel's Calling Neglected

The keen anticipation we have as we approach the book of Judges makes what we encounter in the book all the more shocking. We learn that upon the death of Joshua and all those who had seen Yahweh's mighty acts for Israel, a generation of Israelites emerged who were ignorant of Yahweh and his care for Israel in the past (2:6–10). Unlike their immediate ancestors, who served Yahweh, this generation abandoned Yahweh and "served the Baals," the gods of the surrounding Canaanite nations (2:11–13). And in worshiping the gods of the Canaanites, the Israelites become more and more like the Canaanites in their character and conduct. In fact, one author argues that the theme of Judges is the Canaanization of Israel in the period of the judges (see chapter 5).³ Placing Judges within the grand story of the Bible shows us just how tragic this is. Fundamental to Israel's calling was that they should be a nation distinct from the surrounding nations; but when everything is in place for the Israelites to fulfill their calling, they instead become more and more conformed to the image of the pagan nations.

> When everything is in place for the Israelites to fulfill their calling, they instead become more and more conformed to the image of the pagan nations.

The opening chapters of 1 Samuel mark the end of the period of the judges and the start of the period of monarchy in Israel. The Israelites' motivation for demanding a king further demonstrates their Canaanization. Twice they repeat that they want a king so they can be "like all the nations" (1 Sam 8:5, 20). They do get their king, and as history unfolds, the Israelites continue in their pattern of forsaking Yahweh and their calling. They wanted all the blessings of the covenant but none of the obligations. And because they fail to follow Yahweh, they ruin any chance of becoming mediators of Yahweh's blessings to all nations.

The curses of the covenant (see Deut 28) fall on the people of God as they persist in their idolatry, injustice, and immorality. Over time Yahweh strips back the promises until the Israelites find themselves in exile.[4] In Babylon, God's people are no longer a great nation but a conquered and divided people in a foreign land and under foreign rule. The relationship of blessing seems no more than an ideal of the distant past. Yet hope still exists in this dark time. In this context, the word of Yahweh through the prophet Jeremiah comes to the exiled people of God, reminding them of their calling. The essence of the prophecy boils down to this:

> Get comfortable in Babylon and seek the shalom of the people and place where you find yourself. In the past, I promised to make you a great nation, to give you a land of your own, and to establish my relationship of blessing with you, but those were merely means to an end: so that you could bless the nations. You didn't fulfill your calling to be a channel of blessing with all the promises in place. Now that all the promises of blessing have been stripped back, start acting as a kingdom of priests because in seeking the shalom of your sworn enemies you will find shalom! (Jer 29:4–14)[5]

The eventual return from exile does not usher in the kind of shalom and flourishing that the people of God expected, and they do not prove to be a channel of blessing. Instead, they show signs of becoming more and more introverted and sectarian.

THE BIBLICAL STORY

The contours of the grand story of the Bible, according to Bartholomew and Goheen,[6] are:

Act One: God Establishes His Kingdom—Creation

Act Two: Rebellion in the Kingdom—The Fall

Act Three: The King Chooses Israel—Redemption Initiated
   Scene One: A People for the King
   Scene Two: A Land for His People

Interlude: A Kingdom Story Waiting for an Ending—the Intertestamental Period

Act Four: The Coming of the King—Redemption Accomplished

Act Five: Spreading the News of the King—The Mission of the Church

Act Six: The Return of the King—Redemption Completed

By the time a baby boy is born to an unlikely couple from an insignificant town in the Roman province of Judea, however, God's people had developed an intense longing for Yahweh to return, for freedom, for political independence, for shalom. Ironically, their vision was too small for the Redeemer who was born in a stable in Bethlehem. Jesus' vision of the kingdom was not reduced to a parcel of land in Palestine but included the whole cosmos. His vision for the people of God was not reduced to a single ethnicity but included all nations, tribes, and tongues. And the means of accomplishing his cosmic kingdom was not

> The kingdom that God's people in the book of Judges should have emulated was embodied in Jesus the Messiah.

a sword but a cross—not military might but humility, sacrifice, and service.

The kingdom that God's people in the book of Judges (and throughout the Old Testament) should have emulated was embodied in Jesus the Messiah. His life and ministry, death, resurrection, and exultation accomplished the kingdom and were a guarantee of blessing for all nations. Before he ascended to God's right hand, Jesus commissioned his church to continue his kingdom mission until he returns, when heaven and earth will once again be united and the eternal kingdom of peace will be established. In this glorious kingdom, the nations will enjoy the light of the presence of God and the Lamb (Rev 21:24) and will be healed by the leaves of the tree of life (Rev 22:2).

Reading Judges in the Context of the True Story of the Whole World

Understanding Judges within the context of the overarching story of the Bible makes all the difference in the world. Judges is not just an interesting collection of stories from the ancient past but a chapter in "the True Story of the Whole World"[7]—a story in which we find ourselves today. Yahweh's purposes for the tribes of Israel in the settlement period—for the flourishing, blessing, and shalom of the entire world—are rooted in God's original purpose for the flourishing of all creation in Genesis 1 and 2. God's design for Israel in the promised land is that humans care for and enjoy his world, that his people model a society rooted in the love of God and love of neighbor, and that all people have the opportunity to enjoy the blessing of living under his loving rule.

Of course, Israel is a culturally and historically rooted example—albeit largely an example of what not to do—of God's people living in God's world under God's rule.[8] Yet Judges offers readers in the 21st century a picture of God's intentions for his people and a warning about the devastating consequences when God's people fail to live up to their calling—consequences that affect not only God's people but also the unbelieving culture around us and creation as a whole.

By situating Judges within the context of the "True Story of the Whole World," we can begin to ask: What time is it in the history of God's redemption plan? This becomes a crucial question for helping us hear the message of Judges in the context of our own place in God's redemption story. For example, the church today is not a nation living under the rule of God, yet we are a community of believers living under God's reign. We need to recognize the ways that God's reign is administered differently in the lives of Christians today than it was in the settlement period. To take another example, the wood and stone idols of the Canaanite culture, which continually ensnared the Israelites, are not the idols that Christians in the world today face. However, today's idols of consumerism, moral relativism, and so on are no less alluring and no less destructive to

> Judges is a stark reminder of the serious challenges of living as God's people within an unbelieving culture.

God's people and God's purposes.[9] Judges is a stark reminder of the serious challenges of living as God's people within an unbelieving culture.

But where Israel as a nation failed, Jesus was victorious. Jesus announced, embodied, and ultimately accomplished the kingdom of God. Before he ascended to take up his rightful throne, Jesus charged his followers: "As the father has sent me, even so I am sending you" (John 20:21). As God's people in the 21st century, we too are summoned to do, speak, and embody the good news of the kingdom.

SUGGESTED READING

☐ Genesis 12:1–9; Exodus 19:3–6; Jeremiah 29:4–14; Revelation 21:22–22:5

☐ Judges 2:1–3:6

Reflection

Have you ever thought of the Bible as a single story? Reflect on how the promises to Abraham in Genesis 12:1-3 relate to other parts of the Bible: to the stories of creation (Gen 1-2) and the fall (Gen 3); to the rest of the Pentateuch; to the book of Judges; to the Gospels.

_____

_____

_____

_____

What was the purpose of God's call on Israel, and how faithful were the Israelites in fulfilling that calling?

_____

_____

_____

_____

_____

Why is it important to understand Judges in the context of the grand story of the Bible? In what ways do you understand it differently in this larger context?

_____

_____

_____

_____

_____

CYCLES, SPIRALS, AND CIRCLES: THE STRUCTURE OF JUDGES

The overarching structure of the book of Judges is not complicated. The book has an introduction (1:1–3:6), a body (3:7–16:31), and a conclusion (17:1–21:25). However, patterns throughout the book go beyond this basic structure and show that the book is carefully crafted and deliberately arranged so that its structure reinforces its message. Remember, the Holy Spirit works dynamically with human authors, so paying attention not only to the content of biblical literature but also to the form and techniques the authors use in composing the Bible will help us to better understand and apply the text today.

This chapter will examine in detail the structural layers in Judges—layers that enhance the basic structure of the book. First, we will consider what commentators call "the cycle of judges" in the body of the book (3:7–16:31). Next, we will examine how the series of cycles in the body of the book prove to be more of a downward spiral than just a repetitive cycle. Then, we will identify the many ways that the end of the book circles back to its beginning, creating a circular structure in the book as a whole. Finally, we will consider the significance of these elements for our understanding of the book. Although the basic structure of Judges isn't complicated, the cycles, spirals, and circles can be disorienting. And that's the point. In Judges, God's people are aimlessly spiraling out of control. The structure of the book reinforces that truth.

> In Judges, God's people are aimlessly spiraling out of control. The structure of the book reinforces that truth.

The Cycle of Judges

The body of Judges is made up of six blocks of narratives, each featuring a central deliverer: Othniel, Ehud, Deborah (featuring Barak/Jael), Gideon (and his son Abimelech), Jephthah, and Samson. The body of the book also contains brief references to the minor judges, but those sections stand outside the cycle. These six major narrative blocks follow a general pattern, which is announced in the introduction (2:6–3:6). The pattern is as follows:

1. Israel does "evil in the eyes of Yahweh" by abandoning him and serving the gods of the nations.

2. Israel's actions provoke Yahweh's anger, and he sends foreign nations against Israel to oppress them.

3. The Israelites cry out to Yahweh for deliverance.

4. Yahweh raises up judges who save the Israelites from their enemies.

5. The "land has rest" (i.e., experiences peace) for a specified period of time.

Because this pattern repeats itself throughout the book, it is commonly referred to as "the cycle of judges" or the "judges cycle."

In literature, structural patterns give shape to the text. They're important because they create expectations in readers. Whether we realize it or not, we formulate expectations as we read based on the patterns we encounter. For example, if we encounter a structure of A-B, we might expect that C would follow, but if the next letter is A, we would adjust our assessment of what pattern is at work. An important aspect of reading is responding dynamically to patterns as we encounter them.

Structural patterns, however, are almost never absolutely consistent. Some of the most enjoyable and enduring children's stories seem to follow a set pattern only to upset that pattern at the end. Consider Dr. Seuss' *Green Eggs and Ham*, for example. The delightful surprise at the end of the book—when the main character finally eats and enjoys the green eggs and ham—is set up by the character's increasingly elaborate refusals to taste the dish throughout the book. Many classic stories have a similar structure (e.g., the stories of the gingerbread man, Chicken Little, and the three little pigs). Authors use structural patterns not only to create expectations but also to break them.

What does all of this have to do with the book of Judges? Judges is not merely literature, and it is certainly not a fairytale or fable. It is, however, historical narrative that has been carefully crafted. A good deal of effort went into the arrangement and telling of the events of the settlement period. Paying attention to the details of the literary art of Judges enhances our ability to hear and understand the book's message.

> Paying attention to the details of the literary art of Judges enhances our ability to hear and understand the book's message.

We should further bear in mind that Judges was originally written for a largely oral culture. Today, we often read our Bibles privately and alone, perhaps while lounging in our living rooms or sitting at a desk. The original audience would not have read the

book of Judges at all but would have listened to someone reading or reciting it out loud. Imagine multiple
generations gathering together—whether in the city
square during the time of the kings, around a fire by
the rivers of Babylon, in the city square in Jerusalem
after the return from exile, or in a synagogue—to listen attentively to God's word in Judges. In a predom-
inantly oral culture like Israel's, people would have
been extremely sensitive to both patterns in narratives and the slightest deviation in those patterns.
Consequently, authors during this time were very
deliberate in the way they used patterns of repetition.
The author of Judges is no exception.

What then can we conclude from all of this with
regard to the cyclical pattern evident in Judges? First,
the author undeniably put great effort into structur-
ing his account of the settlement period by means of
the five-part cyclical pattern. The introduction even
announces this cyclical pattern and anticipates that
the body of the book contains six "turns" of the cycle
of judges. Second, like most good literature, Judges
does deviate from the set pattern. Sometimes one or
more elements of the cycle are missing or altered.
We should always assume that these deviations are
deliberate and therefore significant for our understanding of the book. In this way, the details of the
form of Judges reinforce its message.

The Downward Spiral

The recurrence of various phrases and actions in
the book of Judges reveals a cyclical pattern. Various
deviations from this set pattern indicate that the cycle
of Judges is best understood as a downward spiral.

For example, one element of the cycle that appears without fail in each of the six cycles is some form of the phrase "Israel did evil in the eyes of Yahweh" (3:7, 12; 4:1; 6:1; 10:6; 13:1). Israel's evildoing initiates the cycle each time. From this consistent pattern, readers should draw the sad but unmistakable point that the one constant during the settlement period is Israel's tendency toward sin and covenant unfaithfulness. Equally consistent is Yahweh's use of the Canaanite nations as a means of chastising Israel for their rebellion. Thus, in each cycle, Yahweh delivers the Israelites over to their enemies for a period of time.

We see the first deviation from the expected cyclical pattern in the third turn of the cycle of judges. The story of Deborah, Barak, and Jael does not include the formulaic phrase "and Yahweh raised up," though in this case the fact that Yahweh does raise up a deliverer is implied even if we have to wait until the end of the narrative to find out who it is (4:17–22). This element is also missing in the Gideon cycle, but we should assume that Yahweh does raise up Gideon because instead of the expected phrase there is a long narrative of Yahweh's call of Gideon (6:11–40).

The judges cycle further deviates from the norm in the Jephthah cycle. Here, the third element (Israel crying out for help) appears but with unexpected form and content. Up until this point, the narrator has simply stated that Israel "cried out to Yahweh," but in the Jephthah cycle they cry out, confess their sins, and determine to stop serving the pagan gods. This is the first noted time that the Israelites acknowledge the problem and take action to deal with it. However, it seems as though this is a case of too little, too late. Not only is the fourth element of the cycle missing from the Jephthah narratives, but Yahweh actually expresses his own determination not to save the Israelites: "you have forsaken me and served other gods; therefore I will save you no more. Go and cry out to the gods whom you have chosen; let them save you in the time of your distress" (10:13–14). Yahweh does not raise up a deliverer; instead, the narrative makes it clear that the people themselves raise up Jephthah to deliver them. For the first time in the cycle of judges, the fifth element is omitted. This is no mistake but reflects the gravity of the situation. Jephthah was not Yahweh's choice of deliverer—he was the people's choice. Although Yahweh worked through Jephthah (11:29), God's people could expect no peace since they persisted in their evil ways and selected their own deliverer.

By the time we arrive at the Samson narrative, the judges cycle has almost completely disintegrated. The Israelites do evil in Yahweh's eyes, and Yahweh delivers them over to the Philistines (the first and second elements of the cycle). But for the first time, the Israelites don't cry out to Yahweh for help. Do they think Yahweh will not or cannot save them? Do they even know Yahweh exists? Have they simply accepted their fate? The Israelites' failure to cry out should be very troubling and raise serious questions for us as readers. The formulaic language of Yahweh raising up a deliverer also does not appear in the Samson cycle, and though our expectations may be raised by the announcement of Samson's birth to his childless parents (13:1–25), the messenger explicitly expresses that Samson will only *begin* to deliver Israel from the hands of their enemies (13:5). As predicted, Samson has random and small-scale victories against the Philistines, but as a result of his overall failure, the fifth and final element of the cycle is also missing in the Samson narrative: There is no rest in the land as a result of Samson's leadership.

ELEMENTS OF THE CYCLE IN THE INDIVIDUAL CYCLES OF THE JUDGES

	1	2	3	4	5
Othniel	Present	Present	Present	Present	Present
Ehud	Present	Present	Present	Present	Present
Deborah	Present	Present	Present	Absent (but implied)	Present
Gideon	Present	Present	Present	Absent (but implied)	Present
Jephthah	Present	Present	Present (but more extensive)	Absent	Absent
Samson	Present	Present	Absent	Absent (implied but limited)	Absent

Closely observing how each cycle deviates from the expected pattern prompts us to conclude that the narratives of Judges do not reveal a true continuous cycle but rather a downward spiral. In other words, Judges does not give the impression that the reset button is pushed at the end of each cycle, so that Israel starts off in exactly the same spot from which they started in the previous cycle. Rather, with each turn of the cycle, the depravity of the Israelites and their leaders seems to get worse and worse. The cycle of judges appears to be spiraling out of control. The disintegration of the cyclical structure matches what is going on in the content of the book. The Israelites are gradually becoming more and more like the Canaanites, and their leaders engage in increasingly troubling behavior. The author has brilliantly arranged and crafted these events and set them within the cyclical framework so as to reinforce one of his main purposes for writing: to demonstrate the deterioration of Israel in the settlement period.

> With each turn of the cycle, the depravity of the Israelites and their leaders seems to get worse and worse.

The Circularity of Judges

In literature, when the ending of a narrative recalls aspects from the beginning of the story (e.g., events, situations, or phrases), it is referred to as a circular ending. The final section of Judges is unmistakably circular. The author has carefully chosen events from the settlement period that recall and resonate with events from the introductory section (1:1–3:6). The result is that when we, as readers, encounter the ending, we find ourselves circling back to the beginning. There are too many links between the end of the book and the beginning to catalog and describe them all here, but we will look closely at a few of them in order to see the rhetorical dynamic at play.

The most obvious link between the beginning and the end of Judges is the all-Israel war that starts the book (ch. 1) and the all-Israel war that ends the book (ch. 20). These wars frame the book as a whole and are eerily similar: In both cases the Israelites gather together and inquire of Yahweh as to who should lead in battle, and in both cases Yahweh's answer is Judah. The similarities are glaring, but the differences are revealing. In the beginning of the book, the Israelites seek Yahweh's guidance about something that he had commanded them to do (i.e., drive the Canaanites from the land), and the result is failure (1:1–36); at the end of the book, the Israelites seek Yahweh's guidance about something that he did not command (i.e., eliminating the tribe of Benjamin), and the result is heavy casualties among the 11 tribes and the near annihilation of the Benjaminites (20:18–48). The events are similar, but the circumstances demonstrate just how far Israel has strayed from God's will.

A second example is that at both the beginning and the end of the book we encounter Israel weeping and offering sacrifices (2:4–5; 21:2–4), and once again the details reveal the irony of the situation. At the book's beginning, the Israelites weep because Yahweh chastises them for their failure to drive out the Canaanites as he had commanded; at the book's end, the Israelites weep because they've been so successful in their campaign against the tribe of Benjamin, and only afterward do they realize the implications of Benjamin's annihilation. In other words, the first instance represents genuine sorrow over their failure, whereas the second instance represents confusion and regret because they are in a bizarre situation of their own making. In Judges 21:3 they ask, "O Lord, the God of Israel, why has this happened in Israel, that today there should be one tribe lacking in Israel?" This question seemingly places blame on God, as if obliterating the tribe of Benjamin was not what the Israelites had determined to do from the beginning. This example of circularity illuminates the absurdity and tragedy of Israel's situation toward the end of Judges.

The final example of circularity that we will examine is the reference to Jebus/Jerusalem[1] at both the beginning and the end of the book. Judges 1:21 notes that the tribe of Benjamin failed to drive the Jebusites out of Jerusalem. This becomes important in the story of the Levite and his concubine in Judges 19. When the Levite and his company are traveling in the evening and looking for a place to stay, they come to a city but decide not to stay there because it is a "city of foreigners"; instead they continue traveling and lodge at Gibeah, a Benjaminite city. The first city was Jebus— later named Jerusalem (19:10)—and it was only a "city of foreigners" because the tribe of Benjamin did not obey Yahweh's command to drive out the inhabitants; the second city, Gibeah, is an Israelite city, but also one in which horrors occur that one would only expect in the worst kind of pagan city (like Sodom; compare Gen 19). Once again, the circularity here emphasizes the irony of Israel's situation at the end of the book: That night, the Levite and his concubine would have been better off in a city of foreigners than in a city of Israelites.

Other links between the beginning and end of the book also contribute to its overwhelming sense of circularity, including the tribes returning to their inheritances (2:6; 21:24), the applications of the ban[2] on cities (1:17; 21:11), striking towns or cities "with the edge of the sword" (1:8, 25; 20:37, 48), spies and their missions (1:22–26; 18:2–31), women on donkeys (1:14; 19:28), mutilation of human bodies (1:6; 19:29), arranged marriages (1:11–15; 21:1–23), and relationships between parents and their offspring (1:11–15; 17:1–5; 19:1–10). Some of these links are more obvious than others, but the cumulative effect is that as we encounter the events at the end of the book, we're drawn to consider them in light of the book's beginning. The ending circles back (at least conceptually) to the beginning.

Structurally, then, the various cycles of the judges exist within this larger circular framework of the book as a whole. Before we draw together all of the threads of this dizzying structure of Judges, however, we need to consider one more significant aspect of the circularity of Judges that may be easy to miss: chronology.

The Circularity of Time in Judges

As we read through Judges, it's easy to assume that the events happened in the order in which they are arranged in the book (i.e., the events at the book's beginning happened early in the settlement period, the events in the body of the book followed one after the other, and the events at the book's end took place last). This assumption is understandable because that's the way we expect historical narratives to unfold; but in this case, it is an incorrect assumption. For example, it is likely that Samson is the earliest judge, even though his story is the last of the deliverers to be recounted.[3] Also, a reference in the Song of Deborah (5:6) suggests that Shamgar's activity (see 3:31) occurred at the same time as the events of the Deborah narrative. Judges generally omits information that would fix the events to a particular year or time period, and though the notations about the minor judges begin with "After him," this kind of language does not appear in the six cycles of the judges. Though we may have the impression that the events in the body of Judges (3:6–16:31) followed one another chronologically, it is by no means certain that they did.

We can say with some certainty that the events of chapters 17–21 are not the latest in the settlement period. Two easily overlooked details indicate that the events of these chapters actually took place quite early in the period. In a book that generally lacks details to fix events to a specific point in time, these references jump out to us (as they would have to the original audience). Specifically, Judges 18:30 identifies the priest ministering at Micah's idolatrous shrine as Moses' grandson (Jonathan son of Gershom, son of Moses), and Judges 20:27–28 indicates that the events of chapters 19–21 took place when Aaron's grandson (Phinehas, son of Eleazar, son of Aaron) was ministering at the ark of the covenant. By connecting these events to Israel's preeminent political leader and Israel's preeminent worship leader, the author is deliberately calling attention to a specific generation—the generation that was twice removed from the generation of Moses and Aaron. These two details place these events very early in the settlement period and indicate that they're undoubtedly out of chronological order. In other words, the events of Judges 17–21 are an extended flashback to events that happened early in the historical period (which the book of Judges also covers). The end of the book transports readers back to the beginning of the book, completing the circle.

What is the significance of the appearance of these early events at the end of the book? First, the book's chronological structure (or lack thereof) contributes to the dizzying structure of Judges as a whole. Not only do we experience the cyclical/spiraling effect of the body of the book, but when we encounter the conclusion, the circle is completed as we warp back to the beginning of the period.

Second, the book gives the impression that as time moves forward, the Israelites slide further and further into moral, social, and spiritual decay. The final chapters support this impression, recounting some of the most deplorable behavior in the whole book. The realization that these are some of the earliest events in the period should evoke a sense of shock and trigger us to reassess the period/book as a whole. The shocking revelation that these events happened early should prompt readers to ponder how such shocking behavior could have emerged so early in Israel's settlement period.

The answer to this question actually appears in Judges, and this circular portrayal of the chronology of the period should drive us back to the beginning of the book, where we will find the answer. After all, the notations in 18:30 and 20:27–28 fix the events of the final five chapters not to a specific moment in time but to a specific generation. Judges 2:6–10 roots the problem of the settlement period in the generation that emerged after the death of Joshua and the elders who had witnessed Yahweh's great deeds on behalf of Israel. After the death of that whole generation, "there arose another generation after them who did not know the LORD or the works that he had done for Israel" (2:10). Moses' deep concern on the Plains of Moab, as recorded in Deuteronomy, has been realized: Israel has forgotten their King, Yahweh, and their calling to be a holy nation and a kingdom of priests.

This forces us to the shocking realization that Israel did not gradually slide into rebellion and unbelief. The book has been arranged in such a way that we must conclude that they became morally, spiritually, and socially unhinged very early in the settlement period. In fact, the moment they forgot who they were before Yahweh, things went terribly wrong. A pastor friend of mine likes to say, "A people without a memory is a people without an identity; and a people without an identity is a people without a future." This is true for Israel: In losing their past, they also lost their identity, resulting in a grim future.

> In losing their past, the Israelites also lost their identity, resulting in a grim future.

The Effects of a Cyclical and Circular Structure

The cycle of judges is frustrating and seems inevitable. Israel's deliverers gain significant military victories, but they fail to bring about the essential changes that Israel needs: repentance and covenant renewal. The cycle highlights Israel's problem, which is not foreign enemies but a bad case of collective amnesia. The Israelites' failure to remember what Yahweh has done for them and how that should shape their identity guarantees that the cycle will continue to turn again and again. The repeated cycle also gives the sense of a complete lack of progress or goal: After one turn of the cycle, Israel plunges back into the cycle again. We should be impressed with Yahweh's persistence in the face of such behavior, but we may also feel exasperated by Israel's stubborn ignorance. And as we noted, the end of the book circles back to the beginning, profoundly emphasizing the complete aimlessness of Israel in this time period. The cyclical and circular structure of Judges highlights the lack of progress or a goal—it all seems so pointless. What will break this seemingly unending cycle?

Samuel was the last of Israel's judges, and 1 Samuel records the end of the period of the judges. Is the cycle broken? In a sense, yes—but not in the way that it should have been broken. The period of the judges ends with Israel making a request to Samuel: "Now appoint for us a king to judge us like the nations" (1 Sam 8:5). But, as Gideon indicates in Judges 8:23, Israel already had a king—Yahweh—and if there was one thing that the Israelites should not be, it is "like the other nations." Still, Yahweh grants their treasonous request, and Israel transitions to the period of monarchy. This new phase in Israel's history will also degenerate into another kind of cyclical pattern of evil kings (with a few promising kings) who do not bring about the covenant renewal Israel so desperately needs.

> The Israelites' failure to remember what Yahweh has done for them and how that should shape their identity guarantees that the cycle will continue to turn again and again.

Re-Centering Ourselves on God

In his book *Playing God: Redeeming the Gift of Power*, Andy Crouch describes how institutions generally emerge—their development and growth, their stabilization, their inevitable failures. He argues on the one hand that three generations is "the minimum life span for a cultural pattern to be called an institution,"[4] and on the other hand that "by the third generation, every institution has failed."[5] Crouch writes:

> Some institutions, by the common or special grace of God, plant themselves deeply enough in the soil of image bearing that they sustain creativity and flourish in spite of their failures. But others not only fail but die—or worse.[6]

In other words, in this broken world, even the most well-intentioned institutions will experience challenges, hardships, and even failure. But some institutions—those that are rooted in God's will, design, and purpose for the world—will emerge beyond failure to flourish for many generations. Key to the failure of institutions, according to Crouch, are the patterns of idolatry and injustice that exist at the founding of these institutions, which often spell their inevitable end. Institutions that live beyond the third generation do so by exposing the idolatry and injustice at the root of their failure; others simply die as a result of the failure, and still others will continue to limp along in a zombie-like state—neither fully alive nor fully dead.

This describes precisely what had happened to Israel by the time the Israelites took possession of the promised land. They were founded as a priestly kingdom and holy nation on the solid rock of Yahweh's redemption and his *torah* (i.e., God's instruction for Israel, given on Mount Sinai), but the seeds of idolatry and injustice were sown along with the good seed of Yahweh's instruction. The settlement period recounted on the pages of Judges is Israel's encounter with failure (in the third generation from the exodus and Sinai covenant). The Israelites look for a solution in all the wrong places (e.g., military might, political stability) but fail to see the idolatry and injustice that stare them in the face and are preventing them from truly flourishing. The fledgling nation trudges along, not dead but certainly not really living.

New Christian initiatives and institutions—such as church plants, Bible studies, Christian schools, charities, businesses, cross-cultural missions—seem to pop up every day, and many of us have been a part of these. Judges teaches us first of all that beginnings are important. Often new initiatives begin with excitement, commitment, and integrity—qualities that are easy to sustain when things are going well. As time wears on, however, things sometimes go wrong. Failure rears its head, and the excitement turns to discouragement, commitment dwindles, and compromise seems necessary for survival. Initiatives must begin on the firm foundation of God and his instruction. This will not ensure the institutions' longevity, but it is necessary for their success.

> Initiatives must begin on the firm foundation of God and his instruction. This will not ensure institutions' longevity, but it is necessary for their success.

Judges demonstrates that when institutions fail, we tend to look in all the wrong places for the solution. For example, a perennial problem with Christian institutions is gaining support in various forms, such as members, students, and donors. We may be tempted to compromise our mission or message in order to appeal to a wider audience, showing our commitment to the idols of power, influence, and success. Instead, we should evaluate power, influence, and success from the perspective of the kingdom of God, just like Paul did in his letter to the Philippians. The struggling Philippian believers thought perhaps the gospel had failed because they were being persecuted and their great leader and founder, Paul, was in jail. Paul reassures them that they should not count the success of Christ's kingdom by the world's standards. He points out that the gospel is advancing through these unusual circumstances; even in Paul's imprisonment, the good news of Jesus spread to the Imperial guard (Phil 1:12–14). In our Christian initiatives, it is better to see declining numbers while maintaining commitment to God and his purposes than it is to see expansion while compromising.

> In our Christian initiatives, it is better to see declining numbers while maintaining commitment to God and his purposes than it is to see expansion while compromising.

Judges also reminds us that in our institutions and in our own personal walk with Jesus, we can become so busy and so focused on the blessing of being God's people that we forget our calling. Our work and lives can easily spiral out of control and become inward focused or aimless. As God's people, we're called to model God's intention for the world with the aim of blessing the nations. That is our mission; that is our purpose. Our lives will become directionless, cyclical, and out of control if we fail to center ourselves again and again

> Like God's people in Judges, we do not need better leadership, greater effort, or better strategies—we need to stop, repent, and re-center ourselves on God.

on our creator and redeemer and his desire that the whole world flourish. Like God's people in Judges, we do not need better leadership, greater effort, or better strategies—we need to stop, repent, and re-center ourselves on God.

SUGGESTED READING

- ☐ Judges 6–8
- ☐ Judges 1:1–3:6; Judges 17–21

Reflection

Read through the whole narrative of Gideon (chs. 6–8), identifying as many of the elements of the cycle as you can. Pay attention to the transformation of Gideon's character from beginning to end.

_____

_____

_____

_____

_____

Jot down as many connections as you can find between the introduction of Judges (1:1–3:6) and its conclusion (chs. 17–21). How are these connections significant for understanding the book?

_____

_____

_____

_____

_____

Do you agree that various structural patterns in the book contribute to the sense of aimlessness in Israel's history? Why or why not?

_____

_____

_____

_____

Can you think of institutions or initiatives in your own experience that have encountered failure? What was the source of the failure, and how did the people involved respond to it? Will being founded on God and his purposes ensure the success of Christian initiatives and institutions? Why or why not?

_____

_____

_____

_____

_____

_____

_____

"NO KING IN ISRAEL": THE REGICIDE OF YAHWEH

Endings are important. In literature, the goal of reading is to reach the ending. The conclusion of a book is the author's final opportunity to draw things together, to tell us what it's really all about. At the end of Judges (chs. 17–21) we encounter two seemingly random narratives, both of which begin with situations in intimate, domestic contexts but end with far-reaching tribal and/or intertribal consequences. These narratives depict inexplicable and twisted behaviors within private, religious, and public life. On the surface, they don't appear to provide any kind of solution or closure to Israel's problem of leadership, sin, or covenant unfaithfulness. Rather, they seem to provide further and more vivid evidence of Israel's deep problems during this time period.

Chapters 17–21 stand out as a distinct section (i.e., the ending) in the book for a number of reasons. One of the most noticeable differences between this section and the previous one is the absence of the expected cycle. No judges or deliverers appear at all in these chapters. These chapters are also bound together with a new refrain: "In those days there was no king in Israel. Everyone did what was right in his own eyes." This phrase shows up near the beginning of this section (17:6), appears as the last sentence of the book (21:25), and occurs twice more in the final chapters in a shortened form (18:1; 19:1). In this way, the "No king in Israel" refrain structurally binds together the last five chapters of Judges.

The stories in these chapters are long; they include lots of detail and repetition, as though the author, by means of the refrain, is attempting to draw back our focus just in case we miss the point. According to our author, these events must be understood as the actions of people who have no king and who do whatever they think is right.

The phrase "In those days" is referring not only to the time of the events recounted in chapters 17–21 but to the whole period covered by the book of Judges. The author uses these chapters as an overview of the whole period—from the settlement of the people in the land after the conquest to the rise of the monarchy. Of course, these chapters focus on specific events (Micah and the Danites and the atrocity at Gibeah and the subsequent civil war), but they are representative of the period as a whole—they illustrate the kind of anarchy that characterized this time period. This makes it all the more important to correctly understand what the author meant to imply with this refrain.

Human Kingship?

In the context of these final chapters, what crucial message does the "No king in Israel" refrain communicate? On the surface it seems to communicate the simple message that the spiritual, political, moral, and social unrest among the Israelites was a result of a lack of king in Israel, implying that a king could bring about covenant renewal and therefore peace and prosperity. Bible scholar Robert O'Connell says, "Kingship is implicitly endorsed as the means of attaining the covenant ideals of land occupation, intertribal covenant loyalty, social justice and adherence to the cult."[1] Many scholars believe that the purpose of the book of Judges is to promote kingship by showing the devastating results of rule without kings. But does this interpretation make sense against the backdrop of the book and within the historical context in which the book was written? And if the author is not trying to promote human kingship to deal with the problems during the period of the judges, then what does this refrain mean? As we will see, it seems more coherent to understand the "No king in Israel" refrain as referring not to human kingship but to divine kingship. In other words, the author uses the refrain to highlight the fundamental problem in Israel during the time of the judges: They had rejected their redeemer king, Yahweh. The results of their treason are devastating.

> They had rejected their redeemer king, Yahweh. The results of their treason are devastating.

Several pieces of evidence within the book of Judges can shed light on whether the book is promoting human or divine kingship. Judges includes basically three examples of human kingship. First, the book refers to the many foreign kings who ruthlessly oppress the Israelites. Second, after Gideon delivers the Israelites from the Midianites, the Israelites ask him to be king and to start a hereditary monarchy (see 8:22–28). Although Gideon verbally refuses the offer, his actions indicate that he has actually assumed the role of king.[2] This resulted in Gideon setting up an idolatrous worship center, which became a snare to Israel (8:27). Third, Abimelech's experiment as king started with his execution of his 70 brothers and ended with his military campaign against his own subjects (9:1–57).

Although each of these examples offers an image of distorted and evil monarchic rule, they are not necessarily arguments against kingship in general but against ungodly and distorted kingly rule. Yet the "No king in Israel" refrain appears in the midst of behaviors that emerge under the leadership of Gideon and Abimelech: badly corrupted worship of Yahweh (chs. 17–18) and brutal violence perpetrated by Israelites against Israelites (chs. 19–21). It would be illogical to argue that human kingship would eradicate behaviors like false worship and intertribal violence when these behaviors already took place under the (veiled) kingship of Gideon and the (blatant) kingship of Abimelech.

The historical context of the book also makes it unlikely that the author of Judges would propose a human king as a remedy for the kind of anarchy evident among the Israelites. After David's reign, the majority of the kings of Israel and Judah nationalized and institutionalized the twisted behaviors that occurred throughout the period of the judges. The kings set up high places and led the people into idolatrous activities. They perpetrated violence and injustice, and during the divided kingdom, the northern and southern kingdoms of Israel became sworn enemies.

The author and the original audience of Judges had witnessed one bad king after another, which cast Israel and Judah into chaos and ultimately led to the exile of the northern kingdom of Israel in 722 BC and the exile of the southern kingdom of Judah in 586 BC. The note in Judges 18:30 about the captivity of the land is likely a reference to the Assyrian exile of 722 BC, which would mean that Judges was written after the exile of the northern kingdom. This means that the original readers of Judges had probably even experienced the horrors of the exile, which was brought about partly because of the kings' inability to bring about covenant faithfulness and obedience. If the author of Judges were making a case for human kingship, the original audience would likely have responded with: "Are you kidding? Not only did our kings fail to prevent such behavior; they actually promoted and made it a regular national pastime!" Given what the people had experienced under the leadership of the kings, the argument for human kingship at the end of Judges seems highly unlikely. No doubt the original audience would have looked for a different interpretation of the "No king in Israel" refrain.

Additionally, it would represent quite a change of tactic if the author were to appeal for a certain kind of political structure here at the end of the book. All along we have been reminded repeatedly that the Israelites' wayward hearts and rebellious actions were the root cause of the problems that emerged during the period of the settlement. Their unfaithfulness to Yahweh and his covenant kept the cycle going. A mere change of political system from judgeship to kingship would not remedy Israel's malady.

THE EXILES OF GOD'S PEOPLE

God's people experienced two instances of exile. In 722 BC, the Assyrian superpower defeated the northern kingdom of Israel and subsequently deported many of the inhabitants and repopulated the north with other conquered peoples. This is referred to as the Assyrian exile (see 2 Kgs 17). Several generations later, the southern kingdom of Judah experienced the same fate as the northern kingdom. The Babylonian exile began after the fall of Jerusalem in 586 BC (see 2 Kgs 25) and lasted until 539 BC, when the Persian Emperor issued a decree that all the exiles could return home (see 2 Chr 36:22–23; Ezra 1). Yahweh had warned his people on the Plains of Moab prior to entering that land that if they did not remain loyal to him and his covenant, they could expect to be exiled from the land (Deut 28:45–68).

This is not to say that monarchy was not God's will for the Israelites. In fact, God indicated to Abraham that kings would come from his offspring (Gen 17:6). Deuteronomy 17:14-20 also anticipates a time when kings would rule in Israel and provides a basic framework for kingship. This passage specifies three actions kings should not perform (they should not acquire many horses, wives, or silver and gold—

precisely because these are the things in which the kings of the world would put their trust), but it offers only one foundational guideline to follow: The king should be immersed in God's *torah* so that he will know who Yahweh is and rule according to Yahweh's will. Yahweh is not tied to one particular political system; whatever political structure Israel adopts, it must be built upon the foundation of Yahweh's *torah*—his "Manifesto for a Holy Nation and a Priestly Kingdom."

Divine Kingship

Scripture offers abundant evidence that the "No king in Israel" refrain is referring to Yahweh as king. The kingship of Yahweh is a dominant theme in the Old Testament, and the kingdom of God is the central theme of Jesus' ministry, teaching, and activity. Genesis 1-2 emphasizes that God is the great creator-king who establishes his kingdom and relates to humanity, whom he created to live in and exercise his royal rule in his realm. In Exodus, Yahweh acts as the redeemer king by waging war against the usurper Pharaoh and the many Egyptian gods, rescuing his people from their captivity, and providing a constitution for his redeemed people (the Sinai covenant). Countless psalms, particularly those concentrated at the heart of the book of Psalms (Pss 90-106), speak of Yahweh's reign and cast God as the cosmic king who rules not only over his people Israel but also over the nations, the "gods" of the nations, and the whole universe. The prophets also speak of Yahweh's reign, and after the destruction of Jerusalem and the fall of Judah in 586 BC, they prophesy of a coming age when Yahweh will once again be enthroned in Zion and from there rule the entire universe (e.g., Zech 14:9; Isa 52:7–10).

What set the cycle of judges in motion was a generation that emerged after Joshua "who did not know the LORD or the work that he had done for Israel" (Judg 2:10). The "work" here refers to Yahweh's redemption of Israel from Egypt, his giving of his instruction on Sinai, his leading his people through the wilderness, and his conquering of the Canaanites and gift of the land. The Israelites in Judges had forgotten Yahweh—they had deserted their king. Their behavior demonstrates again and again that they were ignorant of the "Manifesto for a Holy Nation and a Priestly Kingdom" (i.e., the Sinai covenant), which had been issued by King Yahweh himself.

The crisis in Israel "in those days" was not merely that they lacked a king, but that they lacked a divine standard for the order of their society. Micah and his mother violate no less than five of the Ten Commandments in just five verses (17:1–5: they created a god other than Yahweh; they fashioned an idol; they misused God's name; and Micah stole from his mother, demonstrating covetousness and dishonoring of his parent).[3] Comparing the "No king in Israel" refrain with the refrain that starts each of the six cycles—the Israelites "did evil in the eyes of Yahweh"—suggests that the events in the end section complete the downward spiral that began in chapters 3–16. God's standard has been eclipsed in such a way that the Israelites are inclined to do what is good in their own eyes rather than resisting what is evil in Yahweh's eyes. As Wilson notes, the first formula "concerns moral action assessed in the eyes of Yahweh as evil," while the second formula "concerns moral action assessed in the eyes of the Israelites as right."[4] The Israelites' doing what is right in their own eyes demonstrates that King Yahweh is no longer setting the standard for life in the kingdom. Ever since Adam and Eve yielded to the temptation to be like God, to set their own destiny and standard of morality, humanity has rebelled against its true King and grasped at human autonomy. This is precisely the kind of treasonous behavior we encounter throughout the book of Judges.

This nature of Israel in Judges reminds me of a song called "The Wanderer," written by U2 and featuring Johnny Cash. It tells the story of a wanderer searching for hope and purpose in a seemingly meaningless world. At one point the wanderer encounters a church where the citizens would gather. The shocking truth about these citizens is that "They say they want the kingdom, but they don't want God in it."[5] I'm similarly reminded of Frederick Nietzsche's parable of the madman (quoted as the epigraph to this book): "He is dead! He remains dead! And we have killed him! ... The holiest and mightiest thing the world has ever known has bled to death under our knives."[6] So indeed there is no king in Israel. Of course, the Israelites would not have dreamed of articulating the triumph of the death of Yahweh, but in this violent and bloody book, Yahweh bleeds, so to speak, under the knives of the Israelites, who have set them-

> God's people want the kingdom—they desire greatness, security, and blessing—but they don't want God in it.

selves up as gods and are doing what is right in their own eyes. Regicide (the act of killing the king) is, in effect, what Israel has done. To be sure, God's people want the kingdom—they desire greatness, security, and blessing—but they don't want God in it.

Recognizing Jesus as Savior and Lord

In 1 Samuel 8, the Israelites see that their leader Samuel is getting old, and they ask him to appoint for them a king so that they can be like other nations. Samuel gets upset by this request, and Yahweh's response confirms what we've just been considering. He says: "Obey the voice of the people in all that they say to you, for they have not rejected you, but they have rejected me from being king over them. According to all the deeds that they have done, from the day I brought them up out of Egypt even to this day, forsaking me and serving other gods, so they are also doing to you" (1 Sam 8:7–8). The rebellious and treasonous citizens of Yahweh's kingdom have rejected their divine King, operating as if there is no king in Israel and doing what is good in their own eyes. This won't be the last time that God's people kill the king who comes to save them, but at this point they are in a bad place indeed and need a Savior, not a mere human king.

We, like the Israelites, are in dire need of a Savior. We, too, must submit to Christ's lordship and let him reign in our lives. I heard the story of a man who had an encounter with the gospel and came to realize his need for a savior. Yet for some time after, the way he lived remained largely untouched by his acceptance of Jesus as his savior. The man recounted the radical transformation that took place when he not only accepted Jesus as savior but also recognized him as lord.

When we relegate God to limited times in our lives (e.g., our quiet time, Bible study, Sunday worship) or to specific places (e.g., home, church), we fail to realize that this is the God whom Paul calls "the only Sovereign, the King of kings and Lord of lords, who alone has immortality, who dwells in unapproachable light, whom no one has ever seen or can see. To [whom belong] honor and eternal dominion" (1 Tim 6:15–16).

When we yield to the pressure of the privatization of our faith, not only do we capitulate to one of the preeminent idols of our day—secularism—but we also drastically limit the worldwide, universal reign of Christ to a tiny sliver of reality. But in truth, it is as theologian Abraham Kuyper says: "There is not a square inch in the whole domain of our human existence over which Christ, who is Sovereign over all, does not cry, Mine!"[7] Similarly, C. S. Lewis writes, "There is no neutral ground in the universe; every square inch, every split second, is claimed by God and counterclaimed by Satan."[9]

At times, the Israelites treated God as little more than a get-out-of-jail-free card—they called on him when they were in distress, but the rest of the time they lived as if he did not exist. Do we at times do the same? In a sense, all of us fall short and are guilty of the death of King Jesus. As the 17th-century hymn goes:

> Who was the guilty? Who brought this upon thee?
> Alas, my treason, Jesus, hath undone thee!
> 'Twas I, Lord Jesus, I it was denied thee;
> I crucified thee.[8]

We are all responsible for the death of our Savior. If we, as his followers, are living as if Jesus is not alive and does not have dominion over all things, may the Spirit open our eyes to the reality of his good and all-encompassing kingship. May we allow ourselves to be subject in all things to the King of kings.

SUGGESTED READING

☐ Psalm 2; Daniel 7

☐ Colossians 1:15–20; Hebrews 1–2

Reflection

We've discussed how the rejection of Yahweh as king is the root cause of all of Israel's problems in the period of the Judges. Look back to some of the stories in Judges to see if this claim holds true.

_____

_____

_____

_____

_____

_____

What does it mean that Jesus is Lord? In what ways have we reduced Jesus' lordship to certain times and places in our lives? Do you acknowledge Jesus as lord of your whole life, all of your time, and every one of your activities?

_____

_____

_____

_____

_____

It may at first seem unthinkable that the church today, like the Israelites of the past, might be living as though God were dead. But can you think of ways that we have set our own standards for certain areas or activities over God's standard?

_____

_____

_____

_____

_____

THE CANAANIZATION OF A HOLY NATION

If the purpose of Judges is to demonstrate Israel's rejection of Yahweh's royal rule, then the central theme of the book is the Canaanization of Israel.[1] In other words, over the course of the book, the people of God begin to look more and more like the Canaanite nations. This progressive decline is only apparent because of the structure of the book—the Canaanization of Israel occurred the moment the Israelites abandoned Yahweh to serve the Canaanite gods early in the settlement period. The Canaanization of God's people is especially tragic because the one thing that God's chosen people were clearly not supposed to do was to become like the Canaanites. They were called to be a kingdom set apart from the nations—to be holy—so that they could bring the blessings of Yahweh to the nations. Instead, the opposite happens, resulting in anything but a blessing for Israel or the Canaanites.

Canaanization throughout Judges

The theme of the Canaanization of Israel is carefully woven into the fabric of the book of Judges as a whole and threads through the individual narratives. The introductory section (1:1–3:6) sets the context for Israel's Canaanization. The Israelites' failure to drive out the Canaanites means that the culture, practices, and religion of the Canaanites will be an irresistible attraction and influencing force on Yahweh's people. Already in the introduction, the author prepares us for the unmistakable degeneration of Israel that we can expect to take place: "but whenever the judge died, they turned back and *were more corrupt than their fathers*, going after other gods, serving them and bowing down to them. They did not drop any of their practices or their stubborn ways" (2:19, emphasis added). The way the narrator tells the story of the "mop-up campaign" (Judg 1) also hints at the Israelites'

THE CANAANITES

The term "Canaanites" refers to a broad group of people who inhabited Canaan before Israel's conquest. This broad designation consisted of a diversity of ethnicities and nationalities. For example, Judges mentions the Perizzites, Jebusites, Amorites, Philistines, Sidonians, Hivites, and Hittites—all people groups considered Canaanites. The Canaanites' polytheistic religion and culture were a constant snare to the Israelites. The Baals (or Baal) and the Ashtoreths represented the male and female Canaanite gods responsible for agriculture and fertility. In Canaanite religion, loyalty to these gods would ensure prosperity and success. This new culture presented Israel with the irresistible temptation to appease and serve the local deities in order to ensure their success in the land.

degeneration: The tribes are increasingly unsuccess-
ful in driving out the Canaanites, from Judah through
the other tribes to Dan.

The progressive Canaanization theme also appears
in the decline of the six major judges' leadership quality. The first three major deliverers (Othniel, Ehud,
and Deborah/Jael) are successful in delivering the
Israelites from their enemies—even if they strike us
as unexpected leaders.[2] In the Deborah cycle, Barak's
hesitancy in the face of Yahweh's expressed promise of deliverance is worrying (4:6–8). The situation
shifts dramatically with Gideon, who verbally rejects
the Israelites' offer of kingship (8:23), all the while
setting himself up according to the pattern of the
Canaanite kings (e.g., using his power for his personal
vendetta, maintaining a harem with many wives, and
centralizing an idolatrous worship place in his hometown; see Judg 8). Jephthah is also self-serving, and he
demonstrates attributes of the Canaanites when he
tries to manipulate God by offering a human sacrifice
(11:30–31; 39)—a practice that is detestable to Yahweh
and a capital offense in Israel (Lev 20:2–5). And then
Samson—who, just like Israel, was called to be holy
for a purpose—is set apart as a Nazirite to save his
people (Judg 13). But like Israel, Samson instead did
what was right in his own eyes: He broke his Nazirite
vow, used his unusual strength for personal gain, and
became ensnared by the allurement of foreign women.

Canaanization in the Israelites' Treatment of One Another

The progressive Canaanization of Israel is also evident in Israel's internal relations. In the introduc-

tion, Israel is a cohesive unit as the people inquire of Yahweh concerning their battle plans against the Canaanites. The Israelites take up Ehud and Barak's calls to arms without hesitation, and they're successful in battle against their enemies. The Gideon narrative introduces the first signs of internal conflict. In the first instance (8:1–3) Gideon avoids potential conflict with the tribe of Ephraim, but later in the narrative he exacts his brutal revenge on the Israelite cities of Succoth and Penuel (8:13–17). Later, Abimelech coldly executes 70 of his own brothers and wages war on Shechem. And whereas Gideon was able to avoid military conflict with the Ephraimites, Jephthah takes up arms against them and slaughters 42,000 men from that tribe.

The Samson narrative offers a twist in the development of internal relations. At one point some men of the tribe of Judah willingly offer up their own deliverer to their enemies to keep some semblance of peace (15:9–13). Unlike in the case of Gideon and Jephthah, where Israel's leaders fight against and slaughter Israelites, here it is the Israelites who sacrifice their leader to their enemies to maintain the status quo.

The motif of the Israelites treating each other like Canaanites comes to its completion in the end section of the book. First, the Danite troops act like mercenaries as they forcibly rob the home of Micah, their fellow Israelite (18:14–26). Second, the similarities between the events of Judges 19 and Genesis 19 compel readers to conclude that the men of Gibeah, in their treatment of their fellow Israelites, are more perverse than the men of Sodom (see Judg 19:22–26; Gen 19:4–11). Third, the Israelites go to war against the tribe of Benjamin and not only wipe out the army but also kill women, children, and livestock (20:43-48). The war against the Benjaminites not only virtually wiped out the population of the tribe of Benjamin, but the other 11 tribes suffered significant losses as well (40,000 according to Judg 20:21, 25).

Over the course of the book, the Israelites increasingly become their own enemies. They were initially called to make war on the Canaanites, but gradually they make war on each other instead. Whereas in Judges 1:1 Israel gathers to inquire of Yahweh regarding who should lead the military campaign against the Canaanites, at the end of the book all Israel (with the exception of the tribe of Benjamin) gathers to inquire of Yahweh regarding who should lead the military campaign against the Benjaminites (20:18). The Israelites have become to each other "Canaanites," and like the genuine Canaanites, they become increasingly merciless in their dealings with one another.

> The Israelites have become to each other "Canaanites," and like the genuine Canaanites, they become increasingly merciless in their dealings with one another.

Canaanization in the Treatment of Women

The role women play throughout the book of Judges adds to the sense of moral decline among the Israelites, thus contributing to the theme of Canaanization. Women are seemingly treated with far more respect near the beginning of the book than they are at the end of the book. For example, Achsah

acts with dignity in 1:12–15 and takes part in a positive marriage arrangement.[3] And later, Deborah and
Jael are noted for their decisiveness in the midst
of battle (4:1–5:31). From this point until the end of
the cycle of judges, however, the narrative treats
and/or characterizes women as either victims (e.g.,
the daughter of Jephthah in 11:34–40; Samson's
Timnite wife in 14:1–15:6) or as people who victimize
others (e.g., Delilah in 16:4–22). The role of women
in Judges culminates with the idol-commissioning
"worshiper" of Yahweh (Micah's mother; 17:1–5), the
brutalized concubine in chapter 19 whose husband
butchers her lifeless body, and the victimized women
of Jabesh-gilead and Shiloh (21:8–25).

Although the founding stories and the laws of Israel
reflect elements of its patriarchal culture, Yahweh's
kingdom is not like the kingdoms of the world even
in regard to gender. In Yahweh's kingdom, males *and*
females are image bearers of the King (Gen 1:27), and
many of the laws in the Sinai covenant afford a level
of dignity to females that would have been countercultural in its day[4]—even if it doesn't satisfy all of our
modern ideals for gender equality. And it is important to note that as we journey through Judges, God's
people increasingly treat women as the surrounding
pagan cultures did—perhaps even worse.

Abandoning Our Idols

In their moral behavior, their worship practices, and
their interrelationships, God's people have moved in a
direction that is opposite from the direction that the
"Manifesto for a Holy Nation and a Priestly Kingdom"

was directing them to move. Their failure to keep the Sinai covenant not only prevented them from cultivating a good neighborhood, but it created a situation in which it was extremely dangerous, both symbolically and literally, to walk the streets at night.

We may easily dismiss God's people in the Old Testament as ignorant and stubborn. How could they be so stupid that they would abandon their redeemer God and persist in chasing after the stone and wood idols of the Canaanites? It seems absurd. However, understanding more about ancient Near Eastern cultures may challenge our critical attitudes. In the ancient Near East, it was customary to worship local deities; these deities were understood to control significant aspects of life like human fertility, crop production, and weather. Those who moved to a new place were expected to identify the deities of that place and worship them so as to ensure prosperity. This was so common in the cultures surrounding Israel that the Israelites likely faced extreme pressure to engage in the worship of the Canaanite gods.

And on top of that, a preeminent and perennial problem has faced God's people throughout history: the challenge of assimilation with the surrounding culture. "Do not be conformed to this world," wrote Paul to the Roman churches, "but be transformed by the renewal of your mind, that by testing you may discern what is the will of God, what is good and acceptable and perfect" (Rom 12:2). The difficulty for God's people throughout history is that we may become so immersed in our own culture that we're not aware of the ways in which it—or its idols—has shaped and influenced us.[5]

If you are reading this from a Western context, it's likely you are more shaped by the idols and culture of the modern West than you may realize. We modern Western Christians desperately need to expose the idols of our culture and the subtle (and not so subtle) ways that we have capitulated to them. Are we guilty of "sacrificing" our own children on the altar of consumerism when we abandon them to chase after the bigger house or the better job? Are we burning incense to the god of relativism when we think that the truths of the faith are only true for me but may not be true for someone else? Have we bowed to the idol of secularism when we reduce the claims of Jesus to our private lives?

> Judges provides a sobering lesson about the perils of rejecting the divine King and capitulating to the idols of culture.

Judges portrays the Canaanization of God's people during a certain time period, but is it any different with God's people today? The idols are different, but the reality is the same. Judges provides a sobering lesson about the perils of rejecting the divine King and capitulating to the idols of culture. May we abandon our own idols and seek to worship only our glorious Lord and Savior.

SUGGESTED READING

☐ Read the Ten Commandments in Exodus 20:1–17, and then read Exodus 19:3–6.

☐ Matthew 5:1–16

Reflection

Reflect upon the Israelites' slide from rejecting the divine King, to worshiping the Canaanite idols, to becoming like the Canaanites. Make a list of the idols of your culture. In what ways has the Christian community fallen prey to these idols?

_____

_____

_____

_____

In Exodus 19:3-6 Yahweh gives his people a new identity. What is that new identity, and how would the Ten Commandments help God's people live out that new identity?

_____

_____

_____

In Matthew 5, Jesus calls his followers to be salt and light. What does it mean for us to be salt and light in the world? How do the Beatitudes relate to this calling?

_____

_____

_____

_____

VIOLENCE IN THE BOOK OF JUDGES

If we take the Bible seriously as the living Word of God, one of the most challenging issues we face as we read through Judges is the issue of the Canaanite conquest. How could God command the death and/or displacement of the pagan nations living in Israel's promised land? This issue is made all the more perplexing because of God's repeated expression that the ultimate purpose of his promises to Abraham, Isaac, and Jacob is the blessing of the nations (Gen 12:3; 18:17–19; 22:15–18; 26:3–4; 28:13–14). How does the Israelites' divinely mandated military campaign against the Canaanites relate to their call to mediate Yahweh's blessing to all nations? Is there any way to understand Israel's interaction with the Canaanites as a blessing to the nations?

How to Understand Violence in Judges

We should begin by acknowledging that addressing the violence in Judges is a very complex issue—one that we will never fully understand this side of eternity. The discussion that follows is not in any way intended to question or doubt the absolute goodness of God or his power or his competency. Rather, we can probe these difficult issues on the firm foundation of faith in God's integrity and reliability, trusting that he knows what he's doing. Christopher Wright expresses the challenge honestly:

> There is something about this part of our Bible that I have to include in my basket of things I don't understand about God and his ways. I find myself thinking, "God, I wish you had found some other way to work out your plans." There are days I wish this narrative were not in the Bible at all (usually after I've faced another barrage of questions about it), though I know it is wrong to wish that in relation to Scripture. God knew what he was doing—in the events themselves and in the record of them that he has given us. But it is still hard.[1]

It's also crucial that we understand where the real issues are and where we have created unnecessary problems. Let me give you one example of the latter. I remember once hearing a speaker argue that we need to have a non-violent reading of the Old Testament— one that actively resists the violent behavior that the Old Testament supposedly promotes. The speaker then listed a number of violent passages, including a clear reference to Judges 19. However, to see this text as promoting violence is a serious misreading of the passage. The narrator doesn't specify that the men of Gibeah's actions were evil in Yahweh's eyes because

Horrors of an unthinkable magnitude result when Yahweh's people reject his royal rule and become a law unto themselves.

this should already be obvious. The underlying message is that horrors of an unthinkable magnitude result when Yahweh's people reject his royal rule and become a law unto themselves.

In an effort to bring clarity to this discussion, we'll start with some statements that will help us to focus on the real issues. The first two points deal with the violence in Judges in general, and the final two points concern the conquest of Canaan more specifically.

Violence as a Consequence of Israel's Failure

After the first chapter of Judges, all of the violence in the book occurs as a result of Israel's failure to live out their vocation as a kingdom of priests and a holy nation. As we discussed earlier, the events of the cycle of judges always start as a result of the Israelites doing "evil in the eyes of Yahweh"—in other words, they forsake Yahweh to serve the Canaanite gods. The abominations of the final chapters occur because the Israelites reject Yahweh's kingship and everyone does "what is right in his/her own eyes." Their evil ways bring them into direct conflict with the Canaanites. The Israelites' faithfulness to their calling could have resulted in blessing for the Canaanites—drawing the Canaanites into the community of Yahweh's people and inspiring them to submit to Yahweh—but instead their unfaithfulness brings about violent conflict and chaos for themselves and the Canaanites. The people who could have been the heart of the solution have become the heart of the problem.

The implied message of the book of Judges is that all of the violence it portrays could have been avoided if the Israelites had remained faithful. This is helpful to keep in mind when considering some of the violent acts in Judges that are difficult to evaluate. For example, we as readers should clearly develop a negative evaluation of the horrors perpetrated against the Levite's concubine (19:22–30) and the sacrifice of Jephthah's daughter (11:30–40), but how should we approach Ehud's deception and grotesque assassination of Eglon (3:15–25) or Jael's brutal execution of Sisera (4:17–22)? It is difficult to determine whether these are acceptable methods of deliverance. But whatever the case, these episodes could have been avoided and are a result of Israel's covenant rebellion.[2]

> The people who could have been the heart of the solution have become the heart of the problem.

So why didn't God choose some other punishment for Israel's disobedience—one that avoided military conflict with the Canaanites? We will never know the mind of God beyond what he has revealed to us. However, both the Sinai covenant and the covenant in Deuteronomy communicate blessings for covenant faithfulness and curses for covenant rebellion (Lev 26 and Deut 28 respectively). Defeat at the hands of foreign enemies and servitude to them are among the various consequences that Yahweh sets for covenant disobedience (others include physical disease, crop failure, famine, livestock illness, and exile from the land). The curses of the covenant would incrementally strip back the promises of Abraham (e.g., to be a great nation, have a relationship of blessing, and occupy the land) so that the Israelites could re-center on their holy calling. They indeed had fair warning about what would take place in the event of failure and rebellion. The important insight, however, is that the vast majority of the violence in Judges could have been avoided had Israel kept the terms of the covenant. Their rebellion put them into direct conflict with the Canaanite nations.

Violence Portrayed Is Not Violence Promoted

The description of violence in Judges (and throughout the Bible) is not an endorsement or mandating of violence. This potentially obvious point is worth emphasizing because the author of Judges rarely provides us with remarks of evaluation. In fact, Old Testament narratives in general often lack explicit evaluation of events, actions, or people. At times, however, the biblical author's judgment is plain; for example, in the lead-up to the flood narrative, Genesis 6:11 says, "Now the earth was corrupt in God's sight, and the earth was filled with violence." And in 1 Kings 3:10, in response to Solomon's request for wisdom, the text says, "It pleased the Lord that Solomon had asked this." Additionally, after David's sinful behavior with Bathsheba and Uriah, the narrator notes, "But the thing that David had done displeased the LORD" (2 Sam 11:27).

The book of Judges recounts a number of violent events and actions, but it does so without affirming these actions.[3] Consider, for example, Jephthah's sacrifice of his daughter (11:29–40). This event is filled with ambiguity and leaves a number of uncomfortable questions: What is the relationship between Jephthah's vow and the Spirit of Yahweh coming upon Jephthah? What did Jephthah expect would come out of his house upon his return from battle? Did he follow through with his vow? And most important, where is God in all of this, and what is his role? We may not be able to answer all of these questions with certainty, but we know God despises child sacrifice (e.g., Lev 20:2–5; Jer 32:35) and that he will not be manipulated (Luke 4:12, drawing on Deut 6:16). God's silence and apparent inaction should not be understood as his endorsement of Jephthah's behavior. As you can see, each case of violence deserves careful attention so that we do not misunderstand what the acts communicate.

Acknowledging that the majority of violence in Judges was a result of Israel's disobedience, and understanding that the violence in Judges is not endorsed simply by virtue of its appearance in Judges, by no means removes the problem of violence in Judges. The real challenge for contemporary readers concerns the divinely mandated violence—particularly violence against the Canaanites. How do we make sense of God's instructions for the Israelites to destroy (or displace) the Canaanite nations? The mop-up campaign in the first chapter of Judges is the final stage in Israel's conquest of Canaan, which is recorded in Joshua and commanded beforehand by Yahweh (e.g., Exod 20:20–33; Num 33:50–56; Deut 20:1–20). How do we reconcile the message of peace and reconciliation that Jesus proclaimed with Yahweh's instructions to make war with the Canaanites? In the coming paragraphs, we will address the question of the conquest of Canaan.

Violence in the Conquest as a One-Time Event

The conquest of Canaan was a one-time event in the history of God's plan of salvation. The conquest was indeed commanded by God, but it was a unique event with a limited scope. Conquest was not a pattern that Yahweh set for his people; their identity was not as a conquering nation. Yahweh's holy nation and priestly kingdom was not meant to be an ever-expanding empire like that of Alexander the Great or Genghis Khan. From the beginning, the period of conquest always had an intended expiration date, and in reality the conquest only lasted about a generation or two (predominately Joshua's generation with perhaps some spillover into the generation after Joshua). Of course, Israel would be engaged in warfare in the time after the conquest, but much of that is either defensive or else flatly condemned as the activity of power-hungry and land-hungry kings.

Before God's people move into the promised land, Yahweh indicates that there are certain pieces of land that he has allotted to specific nations, and the people were not to try to take possession of that land (see Deut 2:4–22). Also, Deuteronomy 20:10 commands that the offer of peace should be extended to Canaanite cities before war is carried out against them.[4] Though

Yahweh commanded the conquest of Canaan, he intended it as a unique, one-time, limited event and by no means as something to be perpetuated beyond Israel's occupation and settlement of the land.

Judges is part of the grand narrative of Scripture. Looking back to the beginning of the story, it's important to note that violence is alien to God's good creation. It does not belong here; it only exists as a result of rebellion and sin entering creation. Looking forward, the story of the Bible anticipates a new creation in which peace will reign. All nations will worship the King, and there will be healing and rest (Rev 15:4; 21:24; 22:2). It is absolutely crucial that we understand the conquest in Israel's history as one stage in the trajectory of God's story of restoration. John Wenham wrote, "God's plan was to select a man [Abraham], and train him to live a life of faith in a heathen world. Then from his descendants to make a nation, whose whole people he might train in the knowledge of himself."[5] Part of that plan involved Israel living out God's intentions for all of life in the midst of a land of their own.

> If the Israelites lived as Yahweh intended them to, they would advance Yahweh's kingdom—not by the tip of a sword but by the nations being drawn into his kingdom and submitting themselves to his royal rule.

The Israelites were meant to conquer the Canaanites, settle themselves in the land, and live according to the "Manifesto for a Holy Nation and a Priestly Kingdom." If the Israelites lived as Yahweh intended them to, they would advance Yahweh's kingdom—not by the tip of a sword but by the nations being drawn into his kingdom and submitting themselves to his royal rule. Seen in this light, the conquest is a kind of necessary evil that was intended as a unique event in Israel's history to facilitate a situation in which Yahweh's blessings would flow to all nations.

But is Israel's conquest of Canaan an act of evil? This brings us to the next important aspect of understanding the conquest.

Violence in the Conquest (in Part) as Judgment

The conquest of Canaan was not predicated upon God's promise of the land to Israel alone, but also upon his judgment against the Canaanites' wickedness. The conquest is not an evil perpetrated against an upright nation; rather, it constitutes Yahweh's righteous judgment on a people who committed wickedness. We may be tempted to paint the Canaanites as the worst kind of moral monsters history has ever seen, but likely they weren't, and not all Canaanites would have participated in their most heinous acts (e.g., child sacrifice). However, their wickedness—both in terms of their false religion and their distorted conduct—is well documented in Scripture (e.g., Lev 18:24–25; 20:22–24; Deut 9:5; 12:29–31; 18:9–14).

The measure of the Canaanites' wickedness had been progressively accumulating for over 400 years. Back when Yahweh originally made the covenant with Abraham and promised him the land of Canaan, he says:

> Know for certain that your offspring will
> be sojourners in a land that is not theirs
> and will be servants there, and they will
> be afflicted for four hundred years. But I
> will bring judgment on the nation that
> they serve, and afterward they shall come
> out with great possessions. As for you,
> you shall go to your fathers in peace; you
> shall be buried in a good old age. And they
> shall come back here in the fourth gener-
> ation, for the iniquity of the Amorites is
> not yet complete. (Gen 15:13–16)

Abraham would not see the promised land, nor would
his grandchildren or their grandchildren. In fact,
Abraham's offspring would have to wait 400 years
until the wickedness of the Amorites reached its full
measure.[6] It is as though Yahweh were saying that he
could tolerate the evil of the Amorites for a time, but
there would be a day of reckoning when their wickedness was so great that he would send his judgment
on them. In fact, this is the reason that Yahweh would
later give for driving the Canaanites out of Canaan:
"because of the wickedness of these nations the LORD
your God is driving them out from before you, and that
he may confirm the word that the LORD swore to your
fathers, to Abraham, to Isaac, and to Jacob" (Deut 9:5).

How Do We Deal with Violence in the Bible?

Understanding the violence perpetrated against the
Canaanites as Yahweh's judgment is crucial. Still, it
shouldn't make it easy for us to accept the violence.
God takes no pleasure in the death of any of his crea-

tures (Ezek 18:32), not even the wicked (Ezek 18:23), and neither should we. Christopher Wright puts it well: "If we place the conquest of Canaan within the framework of punishment for wrongdoing, as the Bible clearly does, it makes a categorical difference to the nature of the violence inflicted. It does not make it less violent. Nor does it suddenly become 'nice' or 'OK.' But it does make a difference."[7]

> We may wish that God had dealt with the Canaanites some other way, but we're not God, and we can and should trust in his goodness even when we do not fully understand his ways.

There's something justifiable and right about our sense of unease at the violence that appears in Judges (and the rest of the Bible). Death, pain, violence—they don't belong in God's creation, and Jesus has become the victor over them. Through an act of violence, violence has been overcome; by means of the judgment of the innocent one, the guilty find mercy. We may wish that God had dealt with the Canaanites some other way, but we're not God, and we can and should trust in his goodness even when we do not fully understand his ways.

SUGGESTED READING

☐ Judges 3:12–30

☐ Judges 11:29–40

☐ Judges 19:1–20:7

Reflection

Have you ever struggled with understanding violence in the Bible? How has this chapter helped you? What questions do you still have?

_____

_____

_____

Read and compare the stories of Ehud, Jephthah's sacrifice of his daughter (11:29–40), and the Levite and his concubine (19:1–20:7). Pay attention to the way the stories unfold, how characters act, and the way characters are described. The narrator does not explicitly say how we're to understand the acts of violence, but can you find clues that help?

_____

_____

_____

_____

Spend time reflecting on the lengths to which Jesus went to defeat evil and violence and guarantee a future age of peace and harmony.

_____

_____

_____

THE ENDURING TESTIMONY OF JUDGES

Judges is not just a collection of stories of far-off times and places with no relevance for today. It is part of God's living and active word, and it speaks as powerfully today as it did in its original setting. But how should we read Judges so that we may hear God's voice and his message for us today? Many scholars believe that Judges is motivated by a desire to promote kingship and/or David and his dynasty. Accordingly, these scholars view Judges as a political book, with the implication that we shouldn't look to it for theological significance. On the other end of the spectrum, some commentators insist that Judges is in no way political and instead view it as a prophetic book that has lasting spiritual implications for believers today.

The challenge that Judges presents to us is that Yahweh's kingship extends to all dimensions of Israelite society—from family relations to international relations, from hospitality to politics. In Judges, Israel's faith commitments affected not only their spiritual and moral realms but also their social structures, family life, method of nation building, and approach to justice and governance. We would benefit from paying attention to all of these.

The People of God Then and Now

Whether we are conscious of it or not, humans are always engaged in the creation and development of culture.[1] Philip Rieff, a 20th-century sociologist, maintained that as humans develop culture they inevitably translate a notion of sacred order (whether express or implied) into an order for society.[2] In other words, the way that humans create, approach, and develop things like music, urban planning, business, and agriculture is based on their notion of what the world is like, how it holds together, the purpose of human existence, the character (including the existence) of God, and so on. The moral philosopher Peter Singer, for example, argues that we should give equal consideration to both humans and animals, and that humans are guilty of speciesism when they put the interests of the human species above that of animals. His ethics develops from his deep conviction concerning the sacred order of the universe in which humans and animals are equal.[3] However, the sacred order that emerges out of the biblical story runs counter to such thinking, instead teaching that humans are created in God's image and are tasked to care for and develop creation, including animals.

The "Manifesto for a Holy Nation and a Priestly Kingdom" was Israel's design for a social order that emerges out of Yahweh's order for creation. The manifesto works out God's sacred order in areas including agriculture, foreign relations, family life, law, economics, worship practice, and social justice. Moreover, it carefully incorporates into its calendar corporate and individual reminders (sacrifice, storytelling, special holy days and feasts, and other rituals, etc.) of who God's people are and what God has done for them. The sad reality portrayed in Judges is that the Israelites begin to use the Canaanites' sacred order to shape their own social order. It comes as no surprise that the Israelites' service to the Canaanite gods produced an Israelite society based upon the Canaanites' moral, spiritual, and social values. Today, Judges largely serves as a warning to avoid constructing our social order according to the sacred order of our worldly culture.

> Judges largely serves as a warning to avoid constructing our social order according to the sacred order of our worldly culture.

Of course fundamental differences exist between the people of God in ancient times and the people of God in the 21st century. For instance, we're not a political entity, many of us do not live in a subsistence agrarian society, and we live in a pluralist society rather than under a theocracy. But like the Israelites, we as the church are called to engage in culture-making in such a way that God's order for the world is worked out in every dimension of our lives. We need to build rhythms into our personal and community activities that remind us of our calling in this world and what God has done for us in Christ. These rhythms should be the wellsprings for lives of public service in the kingdom of God—which, Jesus prayed, should come *on earth* as it is in heaven (Matt 6:10).

As we are molded more and more into the image of our king, the stranglehold that the idols of our age have on us becomes less and less.

Still, we—like the Israelites—may struggle to recognize the things that are influencing our culture-making and culture itself. I wonder what would happen if a group of people from a completely different time or place spent time with us today—went to work with us, attended our church services, shadowed us in our free time, and watched us interact with each other and the world. What would they identify as the motivation for our existence in the world? What would they say is the object of our deepest desires? Whom would they say we serve?

We as Christians face the challenge of being too close to the idols of our culture to be able to perceive them. The result is that we are often not conscious of their influence on us. The Israelites never expressly denied Yahweh's existence or even his rightful claim as the object of worship—rather, they worshiped him alongside the pagan gods or used pagan methods of worship. Are we, as followers of Jesus, finding ourselves worshiping at the temples of consumerism? As servants of Christ, do we more often serve ourselves than Jesus? As citizens of the kingdom of God, have we held back areas of our lives from God, or have we subjected all we have and everything we do to the kingship of Christ? Have we allowed a biblical framework to influence the way we shape culture?

> As Christians, we—like the Israelites—have been called to be a kingdom of priests and a holy nation, submitting all to King Jesus.

As Christians, we—like the Israelites—have been called to be a kingdom of priests and a holy nation, submitting all to King Jesus.

An Encounter with Foreign Cultures

Judges portrays a clear connection between (1) the Israelites' failure to drive out the nations from the promised land (Judg 1); (2) their intermarrying with the Canaanites (3:6); and (3) their worship of the Canaanite gods (2:1–3, 11, 17, 19; 3:6). Judges 3:4 indicates that the Canaanites' presence among the people of God would be a test: "to know whether Israel would obey the commandments of the LORD, which he commanded their fathers by the hand of Moses." Judges demonstrates that the Israelites failed this test. Their encounter with Canaanite culture lured them away from Yahweh's design for them as a nation and shaped their ethics and worship. Again, the problem was not an outright rejection of Yahweh but a synthesis whereby the commitment to Yahweh was filtered through the pagan religion and culture. This helps explain why Jephthah assumed that the promise of human sacrifice would secure Yahweh's favor (Judg 11:30–31) or why Micah thought that an idolatrous shrine with a Levite priest would secure Yahweh's blessing (Judg 17:13).

Today, believers are called to create and develop culture for the glory of God while at the same time being immersed in the culture around us. Craig Bartholomew and Michael Goheen maintain that Christian mission takes place precisely at the crossroads of God's people living out of the biblical story and their culture's story:

> The Christian community living in the
> fifth act of the drama of Scripture is to
> be shaped by its mission: to bear wit-
> ness in life, word, and deed to the com-
> ing kingdom of God. But we are also part
> of a cultural community that finds its
> identity in another story, a story that is
> to a large extent incompatible with the
> biblical story. Since our embodying the
> kingdom of God must take cultural shape
> in our own particular time and place, we
> find ourselves at the crossroads where
> both stories claim to be true, and each
> claims the whole of our lives. How can
> we be faithful to the biblical story here
> and now?[4]

Can we really expect to manifest Christ's kingdom
when we allow our culture to dictate our morality,
our worship, our entertainment, our political sensibilities, and our relationships? Our Christian communities must continually take stock of our mission and
activity in the world, submitting in all things to the
kingship of Jesus. This will require being immersed
more and more into the biblical story so as to live out
of it in the midst of our culture.

An Encounter with Postmodernism

"On a very important level Judges is postmodern in
the strongest sense of the word," writes Carl Raschke.
"The moralism of the Deuteronomic writer ultimately breaks down. God's redemptive efforts can
only be glimpsed if one looks for a more profound,

but far from evident, tapestry of divine movement."[5] The refrain that frames the final chapters of Judges, "Everyone did what was right in his own eyes" (17:6; 21:25), could be an appropriate motto of postmodernism today. However, as Andreas Köstenberger and Michael Kruger rightly point out, whereas in postmodernism this kind of relativism is celebrated, in Judges it is an indictment.[6] In Judges, this refrain in chapters 17–21 contrasts with the refrain in the cycle of Judges—namely, Israel "did evil in the eyes of the LORD." The contrast brings into sharp focus the rejection of Yahweh's standard for right and wrong and its replacement with individual autonomy.

Judges provides a vivid picture of the kind of chaos that results from individualism and moral relativism. It serves as a reminder that truth does exist and that a divine standard of morality does govern human life; we rebel at our own peril (and the peril of our neighbor).

An Encounter with Politics

It may be easy for us to overlook the political dimension of Judges, but it's important to remember that the title "Judges" does refer to a political office. In terms of government, the settlement period begins with a leadership vacuum resulting from Joshua's death. The judges emerge into the political realm in response to a crisis: The Israelites are being militarily oppressed by foreign nations as a result of Israel's covenant rebellion. With Yahweh's help, the judges were relatively successful in removing the military threat, but they did not lead the nation of God's people toward repentance and covenant renewal (as Joshua and Moses had done). Oliver O'Donovan notes of this time, "In the pre-monarchical period the nearest approximation to a continuous governmental function that can be discerned was provided by 'the judges,' and ... they had failed to provide not only the security necessary for Israel's identity but even a consistent standard of justice itself."[7] We can discern different political structures emerging in different contexts in the history of Israel, and it seems that God permits a variety of legitimate political structures as long as the nation is governed according to his sacred order of justice, shalom, and love of neighbor.

Judges provides negative examples for us today regarding the way we should think about politics and governance. Living as most of us do in a secular society, we can find it challenging to discern how we can approach politics in light of Christ's reign. And though we're not called to set up another theocracy, our vote, our engagement in political issues, and our promotion of justice matter in the economy of God's design for us in the world.

Judges serves as a reminder of the perils involved in rejecting the King in the area of politics.

If you don't think Christianity has political implications, consider Paul's summons for the first-century churches to confess "Christ is Lord" (*Christos kurios*; e.g., 2 Cor 4:5; Phil 2:11). In the context of imperial Rome, the only legitimate lord was Caesar, and to confess anything other than "Caesar is lord" (*Kaiser kurios*) was considered treasonous and worthy of a slow and painful death. In any historical or cultural context, remaining committed to *Christos kurios* will inevitably mean challenging the powers of the age. It will also mean approaching politics and power in a way that is countercultural. It will mean a pursuit of justice and peace and a commitment to humility and service. Judges serves as a reminder of the perils involved in rejecting the King in the area of politics.

Judges in Hebrews 11

So far, Judges has provided a largely negative example for Christians who are trying to determine how to consistently live out the kingdom of God today. Can we learn anything positive from Judges? References to judges in the New Testament are rare, but there is one notable mention—one that may at first strike us as perplexing. Hebrews 11 is regarded as a passage about the "heroes of faith." The key phrase in this chapter is "by faith": "By faith Abel ... By faith Enoch ... By faith Noah ... By faith Abraham ... By faith Sarah ... ." In an unexpected turn, the author of Hebrews also says:

> And what more shall I say? For time would fail me to tell of Gideon, Barak, Samson, Jephthah, of David and Samuel and the prophets—who through faith conquered kingdoms, enforced justice, obtained promises, stopped the mouths of lions, quenched the power of fire, escaped the edge of the sword, were made strong out of weakness, became mighty in war, put foreign enemies to flight. (Heb 11:32–34)

The inclusion of these judges in a list of people in Israel's past who lived by faith seems strange, and the judges who are included may strike us as poor candidates. Perhaps we could understand the inclusion of Othniel, Ehud, and Deborah, but surely not Gideon, Barak, Samson, and Jephthah. Was the writer of Hebrews reading the same book of Judges that we have? Did the writer of Hebrews get it wrong or simply overlook the shortcomings of these judges?

The first thing to remember as we address these questions is that Judges and Hebrews serve different purposes. Judges aims to demonstrate the moral, political, and spiritual corruption of Israel in the settlement period. This corruption also permeated the leadership of the time—the judges. The Hebrews pas-

JACOB: TRICKSTER AND THE FATHER OF A NATION

Even before he was born, Jacob struggled with his twin brother, Esau, for dominance; on the day of his birth, he came out clutching his brother's foot (Gen 25:21–28). His life seems to consist of one scam after another intended to secure his prosperity and his blessing from God. And the victims of his scams were often the people closest to him, including his brother, his father, his uncle—he even tries to manipulate God. In a strange story, Jacob wrestled with God himself, and only in his weakness did he experience God face to face and plead with God for his blessing (Gen 32:22–32). God does indeed bless Jacob, and his descendants become the twelve tribes of Israel. Jacob's story doesn't teach us that God blesses those who are crafty and deceitful; on the contrary, it teaches us that God uses broken and rebellious people like you and me—sometimes in spite of their actions and motivations—to accomplish his kingdom purposes.

sage, on the other hand, aims to commend individuals of the past for their faith, which the author defines as "the assurance of things hoped for, the conviction of things not seen" (Heb 11:1). Thus, Judges emphasizes the rebellious aspects of the period and individuals, whereas Hebrews 11 highlights the more positive aspects. The author of Hebrews most likely knew that the faithful individuals listed in the heroes of faith passage are not all unblemished saints. The list includes people like Abraham, Sarah, Jacob, and Moses—each of whom doubted Yahweh's promises, took action to secure the promises in ungodly ways, or circumvented God's will through disobedience.

Hebrews 11 does not present Gideon, Barak, Samson, and Jephthah as paragons of virtue. In fact, the passage specifies that these judges' faith was demonstrated in their conquering of kingdoms, stopping the mouths of lions, and being made strong in weakness.[8] Despite all his fears and foibles, Gideon did destroy the altar to Baal (6:25-28) and put the enemy to flight with an army of 300 (7:1-23). His faith may have been weak, but he was a man of faith. And for all his shortcomings, Samson did stop the mouth of a lion (14:6), escape the edge of the sword (throughout the Samson narratives), and was made strong in his moment of weakness (16:28-30). Hesitant Barak and manipulative Jephthah led armies that did indeed conquer mighty kingdoms (4:10, 14-16; 11:32-33).

The writer of Hebrews is not sugarcoating the four judges in his list, and neither should we. We should allow the judges to emerge in all their variegated colors and allow the clues in the book to shape our understanding of them. If we are completely honest, those we encounter on the pages of Judges are not fundamentally different from us. We often put our own interests above the interests of others and of God. We do what is right in our own eyes. We pay lip service to our divine King and yet bow to the idols of our day. Hebrews 11 teaches us that if people like Gideon, Barak, Samson,

> Hebrews 11 teaches us that if people like Gideon, Barak, Samson, and Jephthah can be considered people of faith, then there is hope in God's kingdom for failures like us too.

and Jephthah can be considered people of faith, then there is hope in God's kingdom for failures like us too. Our faith too is "the assurance of things hoped for, the conviction of things not seen."

SUGGESTED READING

☐   Philippians

☐   Hebrews 11

Reflection

This chapter provides methods of thinking about the enduring teaching of Judges for today. What stories and themes have spoken to you most strongly as you've read Judges? How do they speak to the situations you face today?

_____

_____

_____

Read through the four chapters of Paul's letter to the Philippian church. In Philippians 3:20 Paul indicates that the Christian's citizenship is in heaven, but clearly that heavenly citizenship has concrete earthly implications for the Christians of Philippi, who were living in the midst of a Roman society opposed to Christianity. Make a list of the public implications of Jesus' life, death, and resurrection, as noted in Philippians.

_____

_____

_____

_____

_____

Have you ever noticed an apparent tension between Judges and Hebrews 11? How will you read Hebrews 11 differently in light of this study on Judges?

_____

_____

_____

_____

_____

CONCLUSION

Judges is a tragedy. It illuminates what God's people could have been and then demonstrates what they did become. And however heartbreaking the story, the people of God today need the message of Judges. In Judges we look into a mirror and see a reflection of ourselves and our Christian communities. We see a people redeemed and given a holy calling in the world, a people struggling to be formed into the people of promise and to do the will of their divine king, and a people continually failing in their mission. With every good intention and with the name of Jesus on our lips, we regularly capitulate to the idols of our day.

> In Judges we look into a mirror and see a reflection of ourselves and our Christian communities.

"Do what is right in your own eyes" could certainly be the motto of our modern secular culture, and the church is by no means immune to the allure of this kind of moral relativism. When we serve the idols of our day and rebel against God's will, we not only dishonor the name of our Redeemer King, but we also hurt ourselves and the world we are called to bless.

We will never be done with idols until the return of the King, but the victory has been won. We are no longer slaves to idols but servants of the King, whose face we see in the hungry, the thirsty, the sick, and the imprisoned (Matt 25:31–46). Our King is not like the kings of the nations. As 1 Corinthians 1 puts it, what the world regards as folly and weakness is in fact the wisdom and power of the gospel. May the message of Judges help us to see our King more clearly and motivate us to live more consistently for him in and for this world.

SUGGESTED READING

☐   Reread Judges from start to finish.

Reflection

List three key things you learned from your study of Judges.

_____

_____

_____

_____

_____

_____

In what ways has your understanding of Judges changed as a result of this study?

_____

_____

_____

_____

List any unresolved questions you have with regard to Judges.

_____

_____

_____

_____

RECOMMENDED READING

For a good, short, and accessible commentary on Judges, I recommend J. Clinton McCann, *Judges* (Interpretation: A Bible Commentary for Preaching and Teaching; Louisville: John Knox Press, 2002).

Two exceptional intermediate commentaries are Barry G. Webb, *The Book of Judges* (NICOT; Grand Rapids: Eerdmans, 2012), and Daniel I. Block, *Judges, Ruth* (NAC; Nashville: Broadman and Holman, 1999). For the best advanced commentary, see Trent Butler, *Judges* (WBC 8; Nashville: Thomas Nelson, 2009).

For a solid Christian analysis of Western culture, see Lesslie Newbigin, *The Gospel in a Pluralist Society* (Grand Rapids: Eerdmans, 1989). For a more recent analysis, see Bob Goudzwaard, Mark Vander Vennen, and David Van Heemst, *Hope in Troubled Times: A New Vision for Confronting Global Crises* (Grand Rapids: Baker Academic, 2007).

NOTES

1. Friedrich Nietzsche, "The Madman," in *The Gay Science: With a Prelude in Rhymes and an Appendix of Songs*, trans. Walter Kaufmann (New York: Random House, 1974), 181.

Chapter 1: Introduction

1. According to Jewish tradition, the Former Prophets consists of Joshua, Judges, 1 & 2 Samuel, and 1 & 2 Kings. The Latter Prophets includes Isaiah, Jeremiah, Ezekiel, and the 12 Minor Prophets.

2. Daniel I. Block, *Judges, Ruth* (NAC; Nashville: Broadman and Holman, 1999), 22. The judges are said to have engaged in the activity of judging but are not specifically given the title of judge.

Chapter 2: Judges in the Context of the Grand Story

1. David J. A. Clines, *The Theme of the Pentateuch*, 2nd ed. (Sheffield: Sheffield Academic Press, 1997), 30.

2. Patrick D. Miller, *The Ten Commandments* (Louisville: Westminster John Knox Press, 2009), 276.

3. Block, *Judges, Ruth*, 58.

4. The northern kingdom fell to the Assyrians in 722 BC, and the Babylonians defeated the southern kingdom in 586 BC.

5. My paraphrase with added interpretive commentary, based on the passage cited. Some of the words echo that passage, but I'm giving the essence of the prophecy in my own words.

6. Craig G. Bartholomew and Michael W. Goheen, *The Drama of Scripture: Finding Our Place in the Biblical Story*, 2nd ed. (Grand Rapids: Baker Academic, 2014).

7. Craig G. Bartholomew and Michael W. Goheen, *The True Story of the Whole World: Finding Your Place in the Biblical Drama* (Grand Rapids: Faith Alive, 2009).

8. Graeme Goldsworthy, *The Goldsworthy Trilogy: Gospel and Kingdom; Gospel and Wisdom; The Gospel in Revelation* (Eugene: Wipf & Stock, 2000), 51–57.

9. See Bob Goudzwaard, *Idols of Our Time* (Downers Grove: InterVarsity Press, 1984).

Chapter 3: Cycles, Spirals, and Circles: The Structure of Judges

1. The names Jebus and Jerusalem refer to the same place. Jebus was later named Jerusalem.

2. The technical Hebrew word for "ban" is *cherem*. Cities placed under the ban are completely destroyed. Jericho is an example of a city placed under the ban in the Old Testament.

3. Samson is from the tribe of Dan, and the events take place in locations that are in the Danite tribal allotment in the south (e.g., Timnah and Gaza). This must have taken place before the Danites' migration to the north, which is narrated in Judges 18. As we will see, the events of Judges 17–18 occurred very early in the settlement period.

4. Andy Crouch, *Playing God: Redeeming the Gift of Power* (Downers Grove: InterVarsity Press, 2013), 195.

5. Crouch, *Playing God*, 197.

6. Crouch, *Playing God*, 197.

Chapter 4: "No King in Israel": The Regicide of Yahweh

1. Robert H. O'Connell, *The Rhetoric of the Book of Judges* (Leiden: Brill, 1996), 10.

2. For example, he takes the symbols of royalty from the foreign kings, amasses what appears to be a royal treasure, centralizes power and worship in his hometown, and gets his own harem with multiple wives, which produces seventy sons. Moreover, Gideon names one of his sons Abimelech, which means "my father is king"—a contradiction if Gideon had indeed rejected the crown.

3. J. Clinton McCann, *Judges* (Interpretation: A Bible Commentary for Preaching and Teaching; Louisville: John Knox Press, 2002), 120.

4. Michael K. Wilson, "'As You Like It': The Idolatry of Micah and the Danites (Judges 17–18)," *Reformed Theological Review* 54.2 (1995): 74.

5. U2, "The Wanderer," in *Zooropa*, Island Records, 1993.

6. Friedrich Nietzsche, "The Madman," in *The Gay Science: With a Prelude in Rhymes and an Appendix of Songs*, trans. Walter Kaufmann (New York: Random House, 1974), 181.

7. Abraham Kuyper, "Sphere Sovereignty: The Inaugural Address at the Opening of the Free University of Amsterdam, 1880," in James D. Bratt, ed., *Abraham Kuyper: A Centennial Reader* (Grand Rapids: Eerdmans, 1998), 488.

8. C. S. Lewis, *Christian Reflections* (Grand Rapids: Eerdmans, 1967), 41.

9. Johann Heermann, "Ah, Holy Jesus, How hast Thou Offended?" (1630), trans. Robert Bridges (1897).

Chapter 5: The Canaanization of a Holy Nation

1. Although scholars have noticed the theme of the progressive degeneration in Judges for some time, Block offered a name for it. See, for example, Block, *Judges, Ruth*, 57–59. My work here borrows from and at places builds upon the work of Block and others. See "Further Reading" for more details.

2. These individuals are unexpected for various reasons. Othniel is probably a foreigner, making him a strange choice for a deliverer in Israel. Ehud is a left-handed Benjaminite—left-handedness was regarded as an impediment, and for various reasons the tribe of Benjamin has a bad reputation in Israel's history. Barak is initially unwilling to lead; Deborah is a woman; and Jael is the wife of an Israelite traitor, making each of these individuals unexpected deliverers.

3. Arranged marriages like the one in Judges 1:11–15 may be hard for us to accept. It may at first appear that Caleb is just using his daughter as a prize for a successful military leader. But arranged marriages were a cultural norm in this time and culture that is quite distant from our own. Caleb's actions ensured that his daughter married a strong leader who was brave and willing to answer God's call (in this case, making war against the Canaanites).

4. See M. J. Evans, "Women," in *Dictionary of the Old Testament: Pentateuch*, ed. T. Desmond Alexander and David W. Baker (Downers Grove: InterVarsity Press, 2003), 897–904.

5. The great British missionary and author Lesslie Newbigin spent over 30 years in India as a missionary. After being immersed for so many years in the culture of India and then returning to England, Newbigin had the rare opportunity to see modern Western culture with fresh eyes. He became determined to work out what a missionary encounter with Western culture would look like, which involved exposing the idols of Western culture. For more details, see Lesslie Newbigin, *The Gospel in a Pluralistic Society* (Grand Rapids: Eerdmans, 1989); and *Foolishness to the Greeks: The Gospel and Western Culture* (Grand Rapids: Eerdmans, 1986).

Chapter 6: Violence in the Book of Judges

1. Christopher J. H. Wright, *The God I Don't Understand: Reflections on Tough Questions of Faith* (Grand Rapids: Zondervan, 2008), 86. Wright's treatment carefully unpacks the issue, and I draw from his work for a number of points in this chapter. His discussion is very carefully worked out and easy to read, and I highly recommend it.

2. That is, Israel's evildoing ways caused God to send the Canaanite armies to oppress the Israelites; if the Israelites had not rebelled, they would not have come into conflict with the Canaanites.

3. The first element of the cycle of judges casts the events in a negative light ("And Israel did evil in the eyes of Yahweh"), but we are left to work out from the way the events unfold and the way individuals or groups behave whether we should affirm particular events and actions.

4. Although the peace terms would mean that the Canaanites would enter into a life of servitude, it also meant that they came under the protection and care of Yahweh's covenant.

5. John W. Wenham, *The Goodness of God* (Downers Grove: InterVarsity Press, 1974), 122.

6. Technically, the Amorites were one of the nations of the Canaanites. However, since they dominated the area of the promised land, it is likely that the reference to the Amorites in Genesis 15 refers to the whole population of Canaan; see J. B.

Scott, "Amorites," in *Baker Encyclopedia of the Bible,* ed. W. A. Elwell and B. J. Beitzel (Grand Rapids: Baker Book House, 1988), 75.

7. Wright, *The God I Don't Understand*, 93.

Chapter 7: The Enduring Testimony of Judges

1. Andy Crouch, *Culture Making: Recovering Our Creative Calling* (Downers Grove: IVP Books, 2008).

2. Philip Rieff, *My Life Among the Deathworks: Illustrations of the Aesthetics of Authority* (Charlottesville: University of Virginia Press, 2006), 2.

3. Peter Singer, *Animal Liberation* (New York: Harper Collins, 2002).

4. Michael W. Goheen and Craig G. Bartholomew, *Living at the Crossroads: An Introduction to Christian Worldview* (Grand Rapids: Baker Academic, 2008), 129.

5. Carl Raschke, "Thunder at the Torrent: A Postmodern Theological Reading of the Book of Judges," *Mars Hill Review* 12 (1998): 38.

6. Andreas J. Köstenberger and Michael J. Kruger, *The Heresy of Orthodoxy: How Contemporary Culture's Fascination with Diversity Has Reshaped Our Understanding of Early Christianity* (Wheaton: Crossway, 2010), 15.

7. Oliver O'Donovan, *The Desire of the Nations: Rediscovering the Roots of Political Theology* (Cambridge: Cambridge University Press, 1996), 56.

8. The list of individuals includes David, Samuel, and the prophets, so we can only guess which demonstration of faith applies to which individual in the list.

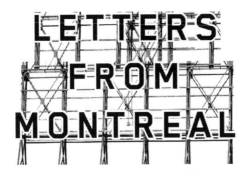

LETTERS FROM MONTREAL

Tales of an Exceptional City

EDITED BY

Madi Haslam

Véhicule Press

Published with the generous assistance of the Canada Council
for the Arts, the Canada Book Fund of the Department of
Canadian Heritage, and the Société de développement des
entreprises culturelles du Québec (SODEC).

Canadä   SODEC Québec

Canada Council   Conseil des arts
for the Arts   du Canada

Cover design: David Drummond
Typeset in Minion by Simon Garamond
Printed by Livres Rapido Books

Library and Archives Canada Cataloguing in Publication

Title: Letters from Montreal : tales of an exceptional city / edited
by Madi Haslam.
Names: Haslam, Madi, editor.
Description: Essays.
Identifiers: Canadiana (print) 20220393370 | Canadiana
(ebook) 20220393931 | ISBN 9781550656084
(softcover) | ISBN 9781550656145 (EPUB)
Subjects: lcsh: Canadian essays—Québec (Province)—
Montréal. | lcsh: Canadian essays—21st century. |
CSH: Canadian essays (English)—Québec (Province)—
Montréal | CSH: Canadian essays (English)—21st
century.
Classification: LCC PS8367.M66 L48 2022 | DDC
814/.6080971427—dc23

Published by Véhicule Press, Montréal, Québec, Canada

Distribution in Canada by LitDistCo
www.litdistco.ca

Distribution in the US by Independent Publishers Group
www.ipgbook.com

Printed in Canada on FSC certified paper.

CONTENTS

INTRODUCTION

When I first moved to Montreal, I watched the sun set in the north. I knew this simply does not happen. And yet, there it was, dipping below the horizon like a shrunken Orange Julep. Only later did I learn about "Montreal north"—how the geography of the city, at least as understood by locals, doesn't align with directions on a compass. The revelation struck me as absurd at the time, but now it feels right. After all, this city follows a kind of internal logic.

The longer you live here, the more that logic reveals itself to you. You pick up on the unspoken politics of sharing a ruelle, or a terrasse, or a paper-thin wall. You learn to navigate the world's most convoluted snow-plowing system. You suffer through a bitter winter only to melt into the concrete by summer. You come to appreciate the subtle beauty of a pothole or a traffic cone. With time, this place starts to feel like an elaborate inside joke. How exactly does this city exist?

Maisonneuve magazine's Letter from Montreal column seeks to answer this question. In 2011, then editor-in-chief Drew Nelles imagined an intimate section that would capture the city's spirit on a single page. *Maisonneuve* may be national in scope, but its identity has always been firmly rooted in its hometown. The column would allow local writers to document the unique joys, eccentricities, and mundanities of living here. The LFM has been a beloved part of the magazine ever since. People often flip to the back page of each issue before they read anything else.

This anthology includes more than a decade's worth of letters published in *Maisonneuve* as well as original contributions from Montrealers past and present. The people writing them are often on the verge of something: a new relationship, a bitter breakup, a big move, or a profound loss. They make sense of those changes by watching how their inner lives refract against their surroundings.

Still, there's an undeniable lightness to these letters. If anything, Montrealers know how to have fun. They make out with strangers. They treat lounging in parks like an art form. They befriend strays lazing on their spiral staircases. They stage bizarre performances in living rooms, alleyways, and old theatres. They are fiercely loyal to local foods: poutine from La Banquise, grilled halloumi sandwiches from Le Pick Up, bagels from Fairmount or St-Viateur but never (God forbid) both.

There's a grittiness to these stories too. Buildings crumble, and every block seems to be under construction. Everyone knows the bus will be late, especially the 80 as it meanders up and down Avenue du Parc. At least one apartment seems to be haunted. Churches and crosses loom over this supposedly secular place. And locals get caught up—obsessed, really—with the symbols and patterns of the city. Old signs carry hidden messages and historic buildings house secret histories. Passersby make lasting impressions however brief their encounters may be.

More recent contributions document a gentrifying city. From Plaza Saint-Hubert to Chinatown, iconic businesses and independent venues are shuttering. The Mile End has become a mecca for tech bros basking in the light of neon signs. These changes are pricing us out of our homes and putting the most marginalized at risk. The letters in this anthology remind us how deeply we are shaped by the spaces we occupy. As those spaces disappear, our culture hangs in the balance. And yet, collected together, these letters also show us that Montreal has always been in flux. Maybe the very nature of being here requires staying open to transformation, both in our environments and in ourselves.

There is much of Montreal that you won't find in this book. You'd be forgiven if these stories convince you that the city exists only between Sherbrooke and Bernard. The majority of our contributors are anglophones stumbling through conversations in broken French. And, while you'll find countless references to the city's colonial history—in the cross atop Mount Royal, in the street names, in the statues—there is little acknowledgement that we are living on unceded Indigenous lands. Most of us are guests here, and this city has long been known as Tiohtià:ke in Kanien'kéha. What might it look like to keep this front of mind as we live here?

Whether you're a Montreal lifer, a recent arrival, or longingly reliving time spent here, this book is for you. Depending on your relationship to Montreal and the era or corners of the island you're familiar with, the city described in these pages may feel like a stranger or a friend. To me, at least, the remarkable thing about this place is just how often it manages to feel like both.

Madi Haslam
Montreal, 2022

Parc La Fontaine Times Two
Melissa Bull

Jean said that, ever since his book was published, women kept assuming he wanted to give it to them up the ass. You know what they say, I said, about making an ass out of you and me. But he wasn't listening. He said he'd pick up whatever girl at whatever football bar on Mont-Royal and get her back to his place—you know, slam the door with your hip, *ma belle*, and mind the recycling bins in the hall. Then there'd be some Scotch and some sofa and some clothes off and she'd turn around and he'd grudgingly give it to her like that scene in the book, at the end. He said that part wasn't even true, or maybe it was true but he didn't even like it that much, he just felt like he had to do it. We'd switched to talking in French, and in French *up the ass* has its own word, a verb—like *bugger*, except people still actually say it—and it's got three good syllables: *enculer*. The *c* and the *l* sound good around the *u*, that French *u* that's short and kind of cute. Sort of between fuck and suck in impact and tone.

We were sitting at the top of the stands at Parc La Fontaine, watching a game of pétanque. Four o'clock sunlight burned my shoulder blades; I'm so white I can burn even in late afternoon. The 45 rattled up Papineau. A lawn mower whined. The pétanque was getting heated. A man with a couple strands of greasy hair cussed out a skinny gap-toothed chick for losing a ball somewhere beyond the tennis courts. She was like Hochelaga-poor skinny, underfed-from-infancy skinny. The whole team had halfway-house faces.

Jean pulled his bag onto his lap. It was a fancy French-from-France brand with a changing mat and a little stuffed animal hanging off a chain. He pulled the mat out to show me. This is for when you want to read in the park, he said. He didn't know it was a diaper bag.

He said, "I stopped seeing the other girls."

He said, "Why are you seeing that Colombian? Don't meet up with him. Come over to my place."

I said, "This is the fucking Bukowski Lawn-Bowling League."

Jean laughed to feel like he could laugh. Like he wanted to like me enough to laugh with me again.

He said, "Is he prettier than me?"

I said, "He's pretty."

Diego met me at the park later. Some wannabe played the theme to *Close Encounters* on his flute, and it sounded tarot-cards-meets-Mulder bad. Why would you play a five-note Spielberg-alien soundtrack in a park? People were still lying around half-naked on Patates Frites Hill, looking like oily fries stuck to the grass. In a good way. In a seeing-people-half-naked-outside way. Even token welfare dude hung on to his chunk of slope, cooling his undecided Speedoed erection and round bédaine in the green light of dusk.

Diego told me about his gig with the circus, how he'd played his lute with wings pinned to his back while acrobats swam in a pool of real chocolate. Diego's face was cherubic, brown. He smelled like strawberry ice cream. He put his mochila, his straw bag, under our heads, and we lay in the grass and held hands, watching the motion of the leaves, listening to squirrels shimmy along the branches.

La Misérable
Chandler Levack

A few months ago, I moved to Montreal because
Toronto was beginning to feel like a plastic
bag tied tightly around my throat. My sublet is
a palatial two-bedroom on Mordecai Richler's
Saint-Urbain, just up the street from Wilensky's,
an inexplicable sandwich shop that keeps drug-
front hours. Our gas stove is an antique holdover
from the early 1900s; you have to light it with a
match. My landlady reserves the upstairs flat solely
for her eight cats and visits sporadically to feed
them and lecture me about leaving the windows
open when it rains. One day, I hang my clothes to
dry and accidentally drop a pair of pants into her
yard, which is below my balcony. I ask her if she
can retrieve them. She finally returns them a week
later. My pants smell faintly of cat urine, but I wear
them out to a loft party anyway.

"Chandler, it's *Montreal*," exclaims my friend
Glen whenever I get nervous about drinking in
the park or leaving our bikes unlocked. Glen
maintains that nothing bad can happen in a city

known for its drum circles and joie de vivre. My third week in town, I decide to bike home drunk in a thunderstorm. It's too rainy to see, and when I turn right on a green light, I am side-swiped by a cab. "Tu okay?" asks the driver as I struggle to get up. When I get home, I realize my wrist is sprained. Things are not working out for me in this city either.

One day, a prominent musician invites me to come drink in a park and says he'll text me when he comes across a wireless connection. He never does, but all night I watch him update his Twitter and Facebook accounts.

I develop a crush on a disco DJ who wears short shorts and billowing oversized T-shirts that make him look like a sexy wizard. One night, at an empty loft party, he asks me if I want a cigarette. We walk outside, and he immediately starts talking to another girl. After five minutes of standing there, I walk away.

In late July, I hook up with a semi-famous comedian at the Just for Laughs festival. We begin a weeklong tryst that mostly involves me walking out of the Park Hyatt at five in the morning. Two hours before the comedian leaves for his 6:40 a.m. flight, I start packing up his suitcases, rolling his track jackets and underwear to conserve space. "I feel like your mom," I say absentmindedly. The silence is palpable.

My mom visits me for a week and we spend most of it fighting. On the last day of her trip, she comes across a Cirque du Soleil demonstration and flies the trapeze. Later that night, we go to a sushi place on Laurier and she talks up a middle-aged couple, showing them endless indistinguishable photos on her phone. When she goes to the bathroom, the man asks me to spend a weekend with him and his girlfriend in Quebec City.

My sprained wrist heals, The Flaming Lips play at the Osheaga festival, and I see God. I try to recoup the unchecked items on my Montreal bucket list: eat at Au Pied de Cochon, walk to the top of the mountain, fall in love. Summer in Montreal makes me feel lethargic and sad sometimes, stunned by too much beauty. My landlord says there is something wrong with me. She is talking about my inability to recycle empties, but I can tell she is also talking about my soul.

In early August, my roommate leaves to film a movie in Baltimore. I light my antique stove and a fireball explodes, charring my face and arms with second-degree burns. I take a cab to the emergency room at one in the morning, alone. "You came to Montreal for what? Your own pleasure?" asks the nurse in strangled English. "Something like that," I say.

The Battle of the Bands
Sean Michaels

I've never forgotten and I can't remember that battle of the bands in 2001. It was a freezing winter evening, one of those April nights when Montreal disregards the spring and fills the sky with snow. I remember this. I remember the wind. I remember ducking into the Cabaret Juste Pour Rire, at Sherbrooke and Saint-Laurent, and seeing a bunch of nobodies make a racket.

We all have our mile markers—moments we look back on to measure how far we've come, how different the light. First kisses, parting looks, the last time the whole gang got together. For me, there's always been this stupid battle of the bands. I do not remember the name of the group that won. Nobody seems to remember the name of the group that won. It didn't matter. The only thing that mattered, in the end, was one of the opponents.

That opponent was Arcade Fire.

Who lost.

"It was the birth of a scene." These are the words of Ian Ratzer. I found him using Google. Ian was at the Cabaret that night; he was in the group that came third, a funk-jam band called Euphoric Side-Effects. He recalls the way Arcade Fire braided Christmas lights across the stage. He doesn't recall frontman Win Butler's cowboy hat. (I am certain Win wore a cowboy hat.)

When I write to Win, he doesn't talk about headwear. But he remembers the show: he had only just moved to town from Massachusetts. It was the first time he performed with his now wife, Régine Chassagne. "The drummer was a kid from McGill jazz school who only played that one show, but Dane Mills was in the crowd and joined the band after that," he says. These are the details that stayed with him. "I think we came in third after two different funk bands." Arcade Fire actually came fifth, as far as Ian and I can figure out. They played country-tinged folk songs. Régine wore glowing deely bobbers.

The reason I came to the Cabaret that night was to see an excellent and funny folk-pop trio, Bear Left. The band's expectations were low, recalls singer Howie Kislowicz—to "play a bigger stage" and reach a new audience. Bear Left finished fourth. "I can't remember the name of the band that won,"

Howie confesses, "and I don't even know if they played another show after that."

They didn't. The winners were a seven-piece funk band that was probably called Gzel Sol but that may have been called Ma Beans and Her Dirty Funk. "We were sort of a late invite—I think another band dropped out," recalls guitarist Sam Sewall. After using the grand prize—studio time— to record a four-song EP, the group never performed again.

Despite Ian's contention that the battle was a landmark event for the Montreal music scene, very few of its participants are professional musicians today. Ian is a video-game programmer, Sam coordinates a chem lab, Howie is finishing a doctorate in law. (His new band, What Does It Eat, released an album last year.)

Win is a worldwide rock star.

None of them dwell on that night in 2001. Only I do. I am the only one who looks back at that battle when he is counting the days, measuring progress. I was there, then; I am here, now. The rest describe it as a distant recollection, a dinner-party anecdote, nothing more. They do not speak of mile markers and how far. They do not sit and think: I am thirty now, a writer, and happy; and how was I before? How was I that time I saw Arcade Fire at the battle of the bands? How far have I travelled?

They are wiser, I suppose, or better adjusted. They have more sensible monuments. It's strange that we don't get to choose.

Death in a French Class
Crystal Chan

The game is the reverse of Never Have I Ever. Each of us shares a story about something we have done, and no one is drinking. You'd think this would make it less interesting.

Wrong.

"I've seen a ghost," one of my classmates says.

Two others hold up their hands, which means: I have seen a ghost too. No one seems amused or skeptical. It's a rare moment of solemnity. Usually the class is filled with quips, jokes, and arguments in halting français.

The first student's story: her family moved into a new house when she was eight. A former occupant had impaled himself after a jump from the third-floor balcony; it soon became an accepted household fact that his ghost made occasional appearances. Behind the shower curtain. In front of the stove. Sitting with you, in the yard, if you were lonely.

"Well," says Ileana from Guatemala, "when I was five, I saw my uncle commit suicide."

"*Se suicider*, pas *commettre un suicide*," corrects our teacher.

"Oui, oui. He was always fighting with my grandmother. Finally, he said, 'I'll never put up with this again!' He ran out. Sat on his motorcycle, then took out the kitchen knife he'd picked up on the way and stuck it into his belly, repeatedly, until he couldn't anymore. Blood everywhere."

"Well," adds the soft-spoken Egyptian our teacher teases for his old-fashioned, chivalrous manners, "when I was nine, I saw a woman die right in front of me. A couple was arguing above. He must've pushed her off the balcony. She splat in front of me. Skull fractured, lots of blood, twitching. I refused to eat for a week, I was so horrified."

"*J'étais si horrifié*, pas *Je suis si horrifié*," our teacher interjects.

Twelve immigrants taking twelve hours of government-funded French classes a week for eleven weeks. Put us in a fluorescent room in Hochelaga and let the psychotherapy sessions begin.

We play another game, this one about etiquette. Some of us can't wrap our heads around the need to show up on time for a dinner party; the rest wouldn't dare arrive late without an apology. Why mince words when it comes to unflattering observations about a friend's weight or age? one student wonders. Others shoot back that it's cruel to say such things to someone's face. Common sense and cultural convention stir together into a thick confused soup.

We also play Questions de Scrupules. It's a party game that would be awkward at parties. Everyone has a card printed with a moral dilemma. When it's your turn, you single out a member of the group and try to correctly predict how they might react to the situation. Example: "You hit a dog late at night with your car. Do you keep driving or do you call a veterinarian?"

I pick a card. Should you accept the advances of a student if you are their professor?

"Of course not!" comes a chorus of voices.

Then, surprising revelations: Javier, a shy Colombian who teaches guitar lessons in his church basement, describes the affair he had with his university professor. Our teacher explains that she is married to a former student.

"¡Caray! We should be careful of her," someone jokes.

"*Câline*, pas *caray*," corrects our teacher.

Il Et It Une
Correy Baldwin

The building at the corner of my block is a mild curiosity. It is a two-storey brick structure, typical of this neighbourhood, although its alley side is painted sky blue. The building has been boarded up for the three years I've lived here, on Rue Édouard-Charles, and the paint in the alley is peeling off, the blue now complemented by the muddy red of the brick beneath.

More intriguing, however, are a number of wood-block letters, white but faded, hung like clouds against the blue bricks. Whatever their message was, it is now incomprehensible. Only four snippets of text remain, part of a lengthier phrase broken up by time and neglect: IL ET IT UNE.

It is French, of course. The letters are relatively small—roughly six inches tall and one inch thick—with exaggerated serifs. (The typeface is similar to Clarendon, according to a friend's mobile app.) The UNE suffered an unknown fate and has been replaced with sloppy spray-painted letters.

IL ET IT UNE—What does it mean? I walk by

that broken collection of conjunctions, pronouns, and articles nearly every day, and the question niggles at the back of my mind. Beneath the letters, someone has painted a white fleur-de-lys, a potent nationalist symbol: four such flowers appear on the blue Quebec flag. Could the building's facade have served as a stand-in flag? Is IL ET IT UNE all that remains of a sovereigntist slogan?

I have begun to ask these questions with more urgency because the building is about to be torn down—and because IL ET IT UNE has suffered recent damage. Earlier in the year, while the adjacent building was being gutted and refashioned into condos, construction crews bashed their way about and inadvertently destroyed several of the letters. All that remains is IL ET (and, of course, the spray-painted UNE).

And so, as a new construction crew moves in, I decide to take action. Late one evening, in an act of vandalism-cum-conservation, I go into the alley and pry off the *I*, the *E* and the *T*. (The *L* is already damaged beyond repair.) Then I take to the internet. First, on Facebook, I post an image of the wall and the three letters I've rescued, asking if anyone recognizes the mysterious phrase. Soon I have a response. "Il était une fois," a friend replies: once upon a time.

What does this mean? On a web forum, I find a useful five-year-old discussion. The corner building, apparently, was once a children's shop, selling either toys or clothes. The shop was called Il était un petit navire—There once was a little ship—after the title of a popular children's song.

Now "once upon a time" makes sense. But what about the fleur-de-lys? On Flickr, I find an earlier image of the street side of the building. It, too, had been painted blue and was decorated with a splash of politically charged graffiti. "Qui est Québécois?" someone had asked—Who is a Quebecer? Someone else responded: "Moi." And someone else: "Moi." In the mid-nineties, with the sovereigntist movement at its height and the 1995 referendum looming, a building painted the same blue as the flag would have been an obvious target. The fleur-de-lys in the alley, I realize, belonged to this exchange.

The building at the corner of my block is a former children's shop, yes. An abandoned, graffitied ruin—that too. But it is also a canvas on which, over the years, the community painted its innocence, its politics, and its hope. A true urban palimpsest.

Now that I know why the letters were there and what they once said, I regret their demise even more. There is a phrase common in Quebec: "Je me souviens"—I remember. Inasmuch as I can participate in this sentiment, I will hold on to my three rescued letters—a reminder of the history of my neighbourhood and of the deeper connection I can have with it simply by looking around.

Where the Streets Have Strange Names
Bernard Rudny

The names of streets and landmarks say a lot about a city. Montreal is no exception. You learn something by walking along Boulevard René-Lévesque and seeing it turn into Boulevard Dorchester the moment you enter Westmount. But our toponymy isn't just about divisions. It also offers reassurance to a city demoralized by scandals. Although the streets themselves may be crumbling, their names show that Montreal's history has always been filled with crackpots and crooks.

Boulevard de Maisonneuve is a good place to begin this tour. The street, along with the magazine, owes its name to Paul de Chomedey, sieur de Maisonneuve, Montreal founder and religious fanatic. To appreciate the extent of his zealotry, consider one episode that's typical of his leadership.

Maisonneuve and his small band of colonists first arrived here in May 1642. By December of that year, they were in trouble. The Saint Lawrence River was rising, threatening to flood the little outpost they called Ville-Marie. Did Maisonneuve scout for a new location or relocate the outpost's supplies to keep them dry? No—he planted a crucifix at the edge of the river, to which he affixed a note to God with the following proposition: Stop the flooding and I'll build you a bigger cross. With a view.

God, in his infinite-yet-questionable wisdom, accepted this offer, and the flooding stopped. Maisonneuve kept his end of the bargain by erecting a giant crucifix on Mount Royal. It has been re-erected several times since, and the current version lights up at night to continually remind Montrealers of God's mercy (or perhaps of a Justice album cover).

Parc Jean-Drapeau, the next stop on our tour, is named for Montreal's longest-serving mayor. Drapeau was a visionary who gave the city most of its modern icons: the metro, Place des Arts, Expo 67, and the Olympic Stadium. They didn't come cheap. Drapeau famously quipped that "the Montreal Olympics can no more have a deficit than a man can have a baby." The games went on to lose a billion dollars. In fact, cost overruns for construction were so high in the Drapeau era that, by 1974, the Quebec government launched a public inquiry into the industry. Sound familiar?

Boulevard Maurice-Duplessis, named for Quebec's populist premier from Trois-Rivières, may be the most inspiring street name of them all. Some historians credit Duplessis as a builder and modernizer. Others decry him as a social conservative with authoritarian tendencies. Regardless, they agree on one thing: Duplessis didn't like immigrants. Especially Italians.

So, when Montreal decided to commemorate this decidedly noncosmopolitan leader, the city took irreverence to new heights and chose a street in the heart of Rivière-des-Prairies. If you've never been, the boulevard is home to many fine establishments like D'Agostino Pizzeria and Sorrento's Bakery, where anyone from the neighbourhood will inform you that it's pronounced "Duh-plessy." "Morris" would be thrilled.

The list goes on. Voie Camillien Houde, the road atop Mount Royal, commemorates a mayor who said that cars "would have to pass over my dead body" before they could drive on the mountain. The borough of Lachine was originally named to mock the territory's owner, René-Robert Cavelier, sieur de La Salle, a seventeenth-century explorer who never did find that route to China (la Chine). And the town of Dollard-des-Ormeaux honours one of Maisonneuve's compatriots whose grand achievement was the failed armed robbery of some Iroquois—an act later rebranded as patriotic martyrdom.

Montreal has always been a tumultuous and unreasonable city. It's the city that hosted Parliament until 1849, when Montrealers burned it down and the government fled to staid and sober Ontario. It's a city that has, for the most part, resisted the boring and businesslike oppression of the grid system. It's a city that thrives in spite of its leaders, not because of them. We may not do "orderly" here, but Montreal will endure. These streets outlast, and eventually forget, their namesakes.

How to Clean a Conspiracy Theorist's Apartment
Erica Ruth Kelly

She didn't sound like a serial killer on the phone. She hired me, off Craigslist, to clean her home near the southeast corner of Parc Jeanne-Mance. I needed quick cash, so I chose to ignore the flashes of Miss Havisham as she led me through her grimy sunroom. Paint was peeling. Small cobwebs were forming. Dust covered everything. I asked her where I should put my coat.

"You'll have to forgive me," she said. "I've been working through a lot of childhood memories recently, of when I used to belong to a Vatican satanic cult."

"Right. Of course," I said, breathing in cat piss. "So . . . should I just put my coat on this chair?"

I followed her through the house, trying to ignore the signs that a B movie might later be made about my tragic demise here. It's funny what you'll convince yourself is safe when you're trying to keep debt collectors at bay.

I asked her where she'd like to start. Closing her eyes, she put her hands in a prayer pose. She wanted to begin by describing the fundamentally flawed sociocultural matrix that our reality is bound by, suggesting the imminent rise of the feminine over the masculine order, and proposing that the food chain is, well, bullshit.

I proposed we start by separating garbage and recycling around the kitchen.

The next few hours felt like an eternity. I swept the back room; she warned me about the Illuminati. I did the dishes; she ranted about abused Disney kids. I picked up pennies and nickels from the bedroom; she channelled my dead grandmother. Her intensity convinced me I was a goner.

Had she poisoned the tea she served me at the end of our first afternoon? "Well, I showed her," I told a friend afterward. "I burned my tongue by gulping it down in fifteen minutes and ran out the door."

"Why so fast?" he asked.

"Because I figure, if she's trying to poison me, I have about twenty minutes before it takes effect," I said. "That way, someone will find me in the park."

My friend warned against my going back there. I reassured him that I would come out the victor should she and I get into a physical fight. She was quite small, you see.

"You know," he said, "the measure of a good employer should not be whether you can take them." He was right, of course, but he also couldn't spot me the money I needed. So I went to her house again two days later.

My survival tactic for our second meeting was to just go along with everything she said. This was not a time for debate. Because, really, who was I to question whether Pierre Elliott Trudeau's pedophilia had been covered up by the Illuminati?

After blackening a bucket of soapy water with remnants of floor debris, I asked the woman if I should come the next morning to finish up. She declined. She was not a morning person.

She cancelled our two following appointments. I have not seen her since. To this day, however, I remain too scared to walk in the part of Parc Jeanne-Mance outside her home. I worry she will emerge and offer me a cup of tea and that, this time, I won't drink it quickly enough.

A Mile End Beginning
Katherine Laidlaw

The first things I noticed about her were the strips of blue fabric tied into her coppery hair—I'd never seen someone who actually looked like their head was aflame. She was crouched on the ground, the rosin bangles that lined her wrists clattering against the pavement. We were both waiting for the 80, the bus that runs up and down Avenue du Parc. It was a sunny Saturday afternoon. The bus should be just another couple of minutes, I thought, craning my neck and squinting north.

When she stood up, her kohl-rimmed eyes settled on me. She held out her palm. Resting on it were a lock and key, like the kind that come attached to the dollar-store diaries of preteen girls. "I've found cards and jewellery on the street but never a lock," she said, smiling. "And a key!"

I reached out to take her offering. I'd just moved to Montreal, and newcomer logic dictates that you never say no to anything, even if that anything is a willowy middle-aged woman nonchalantly offering you a trinket she scraped from the sidewalk. "It'll be good luck," she said before asking where I was from.

Growing up in Toronto, I had always thought of Montreal as a city of visitors—a mythological place with a European air and impassioned politics, yet somewhere you observe rather than experience, even when you're participating. A city you travel to if you want to run into Leonard Cohen or Win Butler. A place where flocks of anglophone university students irritate locals by pretending to smoke and lazily speaking French before migrating to warmer economic climes. Arriving in March, trekking over the Van Horne Bridge in the slush and flat grey twilight, rusting train tracks below, I saw none of its charm.

Turns out, she herself was living in Toronto just then, though she had lived in Montreal for many years and was planning to come back in a few months. She couldn't quite imagine living anywhere but Mile End. "Everyone wants to live here," she said as the 80 pulled up to the curb. I smiled, letting the idea settle around my hesitation. I got on and took a seat halfway down; she stood in front of me, holding a pole. She began an oral history of the 'hood, her long striped scarf falling from her neck over and over as she tossed it back with an air of elegance. Had I seen the flower shop with the white birdcages dangling in the doorway, run by a single mom and former beauty queen? Had I eaten at Wilensky's, the family-run sandwich joint that'd been around for decades? They used to give haircuts but were now open just for sandwiches they made on a grill they'd paid off, a quarter a week, back in the forties. Had I decided which bagel shop I preferred, Fairmount or St-Viateur? She thought I looked more like a Fairmount. Did I know Montreal was immortalized in Richler novels, among others, and was I going to add my own stories to the informal canon? And, most importantly, had I been yet to see a play in that theatre in an abandoned swimming pool down on Ontario Street? She couldn't quite recall the name, she said, but if I asked anyone, they'd know what I meant.

"If you live on Hutchison, we'll be bumping," she said casually as she clinked her way off the bus at Pins. I realized I hadn't asked her name, and I never saw her again. But she was right: about the bagels, the luck, all of it.

The Spirit and the Flesh
Sejla Rizvic

The aluminum-plated spire of Christ Church Cathedral rises high above Rue Sainte-Catherine, though not quite as high as the shopping centres that flank it on both sides. First built on Notre-Dame in 1814, destroyed by fire and rebuilt farther north in 1859, the church is older than Canada itself. Inside, high ritual and traditional Anglican liturgy are enacted in front of intricate reredos, the stone screens behind the altar. At one end of the church, a painted carving proclaims, "Praise Ye The Lord." At the other end hangs a rainbow flag.

As the Sunday Sung Eucharist begins, a small choral group makes its way down the centre aisle, passing by the flag. The building is filled with the sound of Olivier Messiaen's "Les Anges" from *La Nativité du Seigneur*. Light coming through the Cathedral's stained-glass windows splashes soft yellows, reds, and blues across the pews.

The traditional liturgical service on offer at Christ Church reveals the hidden physicality of religious ceremony. By allowing the onslaught of "bells and smells" to overwhelm us, we are more easily able to leave the body behind and surrender the spirit to a higher message.

But the careful, solemn ceremonies performed under the cathedral's gothic arches and wide timber ceilings appear dramatically different in the company of the long strip of rainbow fabric hanging to the left of the front doors. The flag indicates that this is one of the few churches in Montreal where parishioners can enjoy a traditional service regardless of their sexualities, but it also represents an important theological shift wherein the needs and desires of the body are not hastily dismissed as sinful.

During services, the flag becomes a participant—its presence changes the nature of the sacred space. Where parishioners are often desexed and disembodied by entering a church, the flag suggests that the demands of the flesh are not incompatible with faithful worship.

Though the Anglican Church of Canada has a fairly liberal religious philosophy and a mission statement that emphasizes "greater diversity of membership," its attitude toward same-sex relationships has been slow to change. In 2003, the bishop of Westminster issued a "blessing" of same-sex union ceremonies, but the practice wouldn't be adopted in Montreal until 2010, six years after gay marriage became legal in Canada. The ordination of gay clergy, whether married or unmarried, has also been a source of contention. But Montreal's local diocese has decided that there are no canonical impediments to the ordination of gay ministers, and Christ Church Cathedral is now home to two openly gay clergy members.

The role of the body in Christian worship has historically inhabited an ambiguous space between sacred and sinful. The blood of Christ and the holy virginity of Mary both remind us of the vulnerability of our physical forms, their propensity to sin, and their weakness in the face of God's omnipotence. According to Christian theology, the soul is transcendent and eternal and our earthly figures are temporary vessels—and corrupt, dangerous ones at that. At Christ Church, we are presented with the idea that sexuality is not synonymous with sin.

The Ghost in the Machine
Gleb Wilson

L a petite idée fixe is a bar at the bottom of the Mile End. The video lottery terminals, or VLTs, are in the back—large bright computers that are a fixture of many Montreal dives.

VLTs are cartoonish. They appeal to the kid in you. The graphics are sharp and the colours are vivid. You grow familiar with the BAR or the 7 or the cartoon cherry that you might see spinning down the screen. The machine also makes lots of sounds that cheer you on and become Pavlovian pressure points—the clink of money rolling down the coin slot, the computerized melody that accompanies the lines falling into place and sounds like a flashback in a movie, the furious ticking whenever the bank amount goes up.

They are electronic slot machines, a cross between a video game and a broken ATM. Until la Société des loteries vidéo du Québec was created, in 1993, there were as many as 45,000 illegal slot machines in the province. There are now about a quarter of that number, all of them provincially regulated, spread out over a few thousand establishments. Every few years, Quebec releases a new generation of machines, and every VLT in every bar is replaced. This has happened three times. (The last batch saw the elimination of my favourite game, Feu Glacé, in favour of some new games with more modern animations.)

Playing VLTs feels casual. That's a big reason people pour their paycheques into the machines, playing for hours on end, believing in their empty strategies. That's why I'm able to continually hit JOUER and briefly lose track of time. There is a spectrum of fine lines that separate the novelty gambler from the one who can't stop. The one-time gambler, the habitual gambler, and the addict—all of them occupy the same room at the same time, all play the same machines. None believe themselves to be the worst off because they have one another to look at. Only once did I go into a bar alone strictly to play a machine. I felt awful about it and walked out.

A gambling-curious friend of mine once famously put a toonie into a machine after seeing me win a few bucks and screamed when her bank shot up to $500. She hasn't won anything since.

One night at Idée fixe, I introduced another friend to the VLTs. He had never considered playing at all, figured it exclusively the territory of addicts.

I easily convinced him to play a loonie. We picked a game, set a bet, and hit JOUER. We won on the spin and the bank shot up to $8. It felt exhilarating, briefly, like it always does. There was a pause during which he took in the experience.

Later, over a game of pool, I asked if he had liked it.

"Yeah." He smiled, distracted. "It was fun. I was … shocked at how much fun it was, actually." We laughed. He sipped his whisky. A pause. He said, "I kind of feel like we should be playing it now." I nodded.

The machine now had a presence in the room. It felt like someone had walked up to our conversation, and we felt awkward not including them.

The City Undressed
Lindsay Tapscott

I moved to the city in a snowstorm. My heart had been removed from my chest, with the violence of a novice turkey carver, by someone who had told me it would be safe where it was. I arrived an emotional excavation site, but it was a new year. I had Jane Birkin bangs, the air was bracing, and there was snow on the winding staircases when I woke up the next morning. I wasn't looking for a relationship, but by springtime, because no one ever feels "this way about anyone before" until they meet the next person, I was more in love than I'd ever been. Sardonic, erudite—the kind of man who would pay more attention to being called sardonic and erudite than to anything else in this essay—he was a native Montrealer who hated all the things I hated and loved all the things I had moved to the city to love. We spent seven months with each other, our relationship accreting through summer afternoons reading in the grass outside the architecture museum; with olive bread, black coffee, and morning sex in my three-and-a-half on

Beaubien; in the alleys underneath the autoroute at Atwater and Saint-Antoine. He looked at me as if there had never been anyone else. Until he didn't.

He could cook. Like, actual meals: beef flank stuffed with ham, spinach, and red peppers; lemon-and-garlic kale salad with roasted chicken and fresh parmesan. This made the dinner parties we threw in my head a success. He invited me to his Plateau apartment, where we would prepare a meal together that he had shopped for that morning at Marché Jean-Talon. I wore lacy black boy-cut underwear. We drank sparkling wine and made out on his couch. I had such high hopes. He had herpes and lingering feelings for an ex. He informed me of both as I lay spread-eagle beneath him. I got up and started looking for the boy-cut underwear somewhere on the floor.

He was a bartender at a rustic market restaurant on Notre-Dame Ouest. We eye-fucked each other all night. My friend went outside for a cigarette and texted me to say she was leaving. *Are you good?* I showed him the message. "Am I good?" He took me home immediately. I left his place in the near-dawn hours, walking home in the still morning air, past discarded cigarette butts and beer cans on the damp concrete, remnants of other people's terrasse parties. Caught up in my post-drunken haze, it took me hours to notice that my apartment had been broken into. I'd been so focused on what I'd gained.

On our first date, he took me to a bar inside the Place des Arts complex. He said he'd read great reviews. We walked into an almost-empty roped-off area of a theatre lobby, the kind with burgundy carpeting where you make small talk with your mom during intermission. Once we'd stopped laughing, I insisted we stay for one drink. Afterward, I took him to a small low-lit wine bar at Parc and Sherbrooke and he told me about investment funds. He brought me to an Arcade Fire show, then backstage to meet Win Butler because they played basketball together. I would later learn that he thought this would impress me. He bought me ice cream and kissed me in the parking lot. We dated for about a month, but when we had met, I was already halfway out of the city—the lack of work had worn thin. He tried to persuade me to stay, but the truth is, I was already gone. No boy could touch me.

Old Haunts
Haley Cullingham

My mum got into a cab at Trudeau and asked the driver to take her to the Mile End. They had pulled off the highway before she directed him to my house. He shook his head when she finished. "No," he said. "That's not where she lives."

"I think I know my daughter's address," she responded, fumbling with her cellphone to confirm the house number.

"That's not where your daughter lives," he repeated, sure of himself. "That's my ex-wife's gynecologist."

The floors of the front two bedrooms were, indeed, tiled. Above my roommate Noah's mattress, the runner for an old surgical curtain still had the hooks attached. Rumour had it that the doctor had set up his deathbed in the circular living room with I-Can't-Believe-It's-Not-Butter-coloured walls. In the unfinished basement, Noah found books on abortion from the 1900s. It was a three-minute walk to the Morgentaler Clinic.

The night I moved in, I heard a group of my roommate Natasha's friends discuss a plan to cleanse the house of evil spirits. The stereo used to turn off by itself, they said. Once, Natasha woke up and saw two angry figures at the end of her bed. A week later, she was sitting on the couch with her friend Émilie and they both felt a chill. They gathered up their wine and hightailed it to the safety of the mountain. Plates would fly out of hands despite a firm grip. Noah's cat, Serge, would charge at bedroom doors, chasing things none of us could see.

Our landlady was an older woman whom we knew only by a hyphenated last name. She insisted on picking up four individual cheques from us every month and would brusque into the house in a skirt suit to collect them from the kitchen. She regarded us in descending order of interest based on our grasp of French. Her boyfriend, or maybe her brother, was friendlier. White haired and affable, he was called in if something broke. The offending fixture would languish unmended for weeks until he came to repair it, always stopping two steps shy of finished. We turned the shower on with a wrench instead of a tap. There was a little diagram taped to the stove to indicate which burners were stuck on high and which didn't work at all. "I don't own the house," our landlady told Noah when the furnace broke. "The rent doesn't even go to me." It took them weeks to turn the heat back on. I scraped frost off the inside of my window with my fingernails.

One morning after we hosted a Halloween party, Noah took his cup of coffee out to the disintegrating wicker chairs on the porch. A man about our age was poking around the property. "Did you leave something here last night?" Noah asked.

The man looked at him, startled. "My father used to live here," he said.

His dad had been a doctor and had died when he was only five years old. The lawyers had caught his stepmother trying to alter his father's will, and she had managed to convince them to leave the house in her care until her stepson was old enough to manage it. Even though he wasn't technically allowed on the property until it changed hands, he wanted to come check it out. He told Noah that he had a feeling she wasn't keeping it up.

He described what he remembered of the house from childhood. The mounds of dirt at the back of the shadowy basement, still unchanged. The layout. "That room on the left, that was the waiting room," he said, gesturing to Natasha's window.

"On the right was examinations." Patients used to convalesce in my bedroom at the back, behind the kitchen. He didn't mention his dad setting up his deathbed where we kept our coffee table.

He would get the keys when he turned thirty, he told Noah. By then, we'd all have moved out. The house didn't belong to us, and it didn't belong to him either. Or to the landlady. The house belonged to the ghosts.

Under the Paifang
Jessica Wei

Before there was a China, in my mind, there was Montreal's Chinatown. It's a yellowed photograph from the seventies: among cobbled streets and brick buildings, a girl with bright eyes—my mom, increasingly younger than me—stands with her mother in their first winter coats. Another picture shows them, along with my father, in front of the grand red arches with golden tiles and a curved horizontal beam. I've walked under these gates to the neighbourhood, covered with tiles that my parents imported from Taiwan, countless times. Sometimes it feels like I'm accessing a piece of my past just by stopping at the butcher for a pound of barbecued pork or eating at Restaurant Hong Kong, where I'm greeted by a friendly manager who has always looked like an old uncle. But, most of the time, it just feels like I'm going grocery shopping or eating pretty good Chinese food ordered off the English part of the menu.

My parents moved to Montreal from Taipei and Hong Kong when they were eighteen and nineteen. They met at a Chinese church and formed a community with other immigrants, trading job leads during Bible study before going for hot pot. Neither had attended university, so my mom took business classes at night while my dad worked. On quiet evenings, he'd pick her up after class and they would trudge home in the snow together, stopping at a Vietnamese-run video store to pick up the latest Hong Kong blockbusters.

Back then, Chinatown was a collection of restaurants and small grocery-and-import stores staffed by Cantonese speakers who took smoke breaks in one another's kitchens. Because my dad spoke English, he waited tables at Restaurant Hunan. My mom kept the books at her parents' importing company. They shipped goods from Taiwan into Chinatown grocery stores and then expanded into decorations: wooden dragons, china tile, and gold wall ornaments for restaurants all over the city. Chinatown bloomed into a cultural centre and tourist destination, and soon the architect in charge of redesigning the area hired my mother to secure the iconic red tiles for the paifang at the corner of René-Lévesque (then Boulevard Dorchester) and Saint-Laurent.

At the height of their success, my parents ran three gift shops across the city. They spoke Cantonese more than English. Their French was almost nonexistent save for the odd "Bon-joo" and "Meh-ci" when talking to francophone customers. They ate at their friends' restaurants, places with two menus that turned out decent, cheap hangover food to sai yun (Westerners) as well as reminders of something like home for more familiar patrons. Soon my parents had my brother and me, moved to the suburbs and then to Toronto in search of better jobs, relief from the pre-referendum climate and a school system that didn't impose yet another language between immigrant parents and their kids.

Eventually, I returned to Montreal, where I have hustled too. Between tutoring jobs, call centres, and cafés, I've been peddling articles and editing others'. On quiet nights, my boyfriend meets me after work and we trudge home in the snow to watch Cantonese dramas. We talk shop over our little hot pot burner. I pass the gates of Chinatown weekly to get groceries, often not even noticing the dusty ink-red tiles. I'm pretty sure the manager of Restaurant Hong Kong has pinched my cheeks, but it was decades ago, so he now passes me the English menu. I wonder if he remembers my parents, those two young schemers who used to scarf down yeung chow fried rice and plates of gai lan between shifts at work.

I talk about moving to Hong Kong to try my

hand at a different kind of hustling—one intrinsically linked to the inherent privilege to wander as opposed to the necessity of finding a life that is more amenable to one's needs. I could learn how to read the language of my native tongue, come back a "real Chinese." Hong Kong is bigger and more exciting than the handful of blocks that make up Chinatown, but there is a certain comfort in this neighbourhood caught between cultures. Fragments of my parents' past are strewn all over the city, little chapters of their brave, ambitious, impecunious youth. They follow me around cobbled corners, from restaurant to grocery store, all the way home.

Catching the Light
Sara Black McCulloch

Once, my grandmother and I got lost. We stood under a willow, the sunlight tickling its long strands, the light flickering. My yaya told me she couldn't remember the way. I was distracted less by the prospect of never finding home than by the towering willow letting the light in, allowing it to brighten or dull its green.

When I was young, my yaya and I would hop on the 16 from Ville Saint-Laurent to Parc-Ex. In between running errands, we would take breaks on the benches in intermittent parks. We would sit and enjoy the silence together. She would hug me, and off we would go to a bakery to pick up spanakopita or to her friend's house to eat molasses cookies. I remember the thaw, the slush, and the sudden burst of sunlight in the afternoons.

My grandmother died when I was thirteen. For a long time, I couldn't walk by our familiar spots without wanting to cry. Greeks mourn differently. We hold vigils in church at every anniversary so that we don't forget the person we've lost. Now,

I hold similar vigils as I tread the paths I once walked with my grandmother. I remember more and more about her and how those walks allowed me to feel comfortable in silence.

But it's getting harder because so much has changed. The storefronts are abandoned or sold. The pastry shops have shut down and the friends have migrated to Laval.

When Virginia Woolf went for walks, it was to give some order to her thoughts. Moving her body was a way she could settle her mind. I walk to do the same. Tracing familiar streets helps me remember and connect to certain parts of myself. I walk along Parc and it helps ground me, especially when I've forgotten so much.

Spring comes right when I'm used to the cold: my skin, trapped beneath layers of wool and thermal cotton, anticipates an ambush from the wind. When the chill disappears, it's all too sudden. I'm frantically catching up. Things surface on sidewalks, trees start budding, and houseplants angle toward the windows, trying to capture light. Spring is a signifier for renewal, and I begin to remember certain things. Little memories resurface. I replay them in my head as though the repetition will cement them.

I'm in a fog when I leave my apartment. The sheets of ice laid down by winter are melting, and the ground isn't as stable. I shiver and slip on a puddle that's still partially frozen. I'm stuck in my head, preoccupied by deadlines, writer's block, and friends, and soon I realize I've walked too far. I've forgotten the anniversary of my grandmother's death.

The willow tree still stands in Ville Saint-Laurent— so close to where my grandmother helped raise me. So much around it has changed: houses have been demolished and renovated, our favourite diner too. The willow is there when I walk home at night, after I've missed the last bus, but it doesn't calm me anymore. When I look up at its branches, I no longer remember the strong, protective presence of my grandmother. I remember the feeling of change, of forgetting. I'm scared that, if the conditions are right, if the light ever matches my memory of that day when we weren't sure we would find our way home, I won't even notice. I'll just keep walking.

Les Enfants du Roi
Deborah Ostrovsky

To get to my library's Baby Rhyme and Story Time, my daughter and I have to open the front door, walk to the corner of Avenue Mont-Royal, and cross the street. Even when the ice on the sidewalk freezes into thick, wavy layers, the trip should take five minutes. Toddler tantrums, however, can make the journey last thirty, whether we're in boots or sandals.

Witnessing an urban child freak-out is rare in the Plateau. Not because there aren't kids. As my daughter weeps and stomps, the sidewalks spill over with kick scooters and balance bikes. Curly-headed cherubs lounge in strollers pushed by tattooed, bearded dads. No, it is a matter of demographics. Many here are from France; about 100,000 French expats live in Montreal, 20,000 of whom call my neighbourhood home. "La petite France" is overrun with elegant, polite French children. They greet guests upon entering a room and recite thank yous without prompting. These refined, cultured adults stuffed inside two-foot frames make cameo appearances in bakeries, exhibiting an uncanny amount of self-control—no holding mothers hostage at the register, demanding viennoiseries. At parties, they eat raw cheeses with slimy rinds that could curl the tongues of even the most epicurean Canadian adults; at swimming classes on Avenue Papineau, they shiver, blue with cold but responding to instructions without dragging their flip-flops or, like my own daughter, letting out blood-curdling screams.

There is a difference between how French and Canadian parents raise their children: le cadre. In *Bringing Up Bébé*, American-born and Paris-based Pamela Druckerman explains the term, "frame" in English, as the boundaries and rules the children learn. I've performed many a late-night exegesis on Druckerman's book about how French child rearing, like French cuisine and French art galleries, is superior.

But what I have witnessed in my corner of Montreal is identical to Druckerman's description of behaviour in Paris and Strasbourg.

To the untrained eye, French parents may appear disengaged. Spend a Wednesday evening at the Gilles-Lefebvre playground and you'll see them arrive after work in polished black pumps and white linen slacks, reading *Le Monde* or chattering with friends while their offspring play on their own. Their kids have learned not to be enfants-rois; they entertain themselves. Meanwhile, my fingers hover over 911 as I nervously track my daughter through the jungle gym wearing sweatpants stained with egg from yesterday's breakfast.

My friend Marie, originally from Saint-Malo, says French society has higher expectations of maturity in children. Marie has been getting gussied up for full-course meals at restaurants since the age of three. She sees children doing the same today at her parents' hotel in Brittany. But, while working at an upscale bistro in Outremont, she looked on in disbelief as Canadian tots watched cartoons on their iPads over appetizers. "They won't eat oysters," she laments while leaning against my kitchen counter, watching as I cook another white-pasta kiddie meal.

It is always a relief, though, to see that children can still act like children no matter where they are from. One afternoon last January, I witnessed the four-year-old son of a Toulousaine acquaintance have a meltdown at a café near Parc La Fontaine. It was almost nap time, and exhausted from an afternoon of sledding, the boy writhed around on a couch, then on the floor, screaming. Standing there, a grown woman watching a child screech and pound, I felt smug. I felt satisfied. Finally, brats from the land of liberté, egalité, et fraternité.

As the boy's shrieks continued, another friend's daughter—this one from Brittany and barely three years old—approached. The tiny girl handed him a piece of chocolate marble cake from a linen cloth, calming the boy immediately. Having solved the problem, she turned to offer me a slice too.

"C'est délicieux," I said, taking a bite. "Did your mommy make it?"

The little girl looked up at me, confused.

"Non, pas du tout," her mother interjected, pointing back at her daughter. "She did." She said it without boastfulness, without gloating, and they both went back to eating their cake. C'est rien.

As the Snow Flies
Mim Kempson

It was a November afternoon when I first saw confetti falling from the sky. I was sitting in a café off Avenue Mont-Royal and I peered at the other patrons, assuming they'd share my bewilderment. They did not. My friend Sarah, who happened to be the barista, joined me as I rushed outside. Out on the sun-bathed street, I marvelled at the glittery specks that fell onto my face. "Félicitations," Sarah exclaimed. "C'est ta première neige!"

In the months before I moved from Melbourne to Montreal, the technicalities of winter were often on my mind. My experience with snow was limited to Hollywood movie sets and news stories about polar vortexes. I had many questions: How do you walk without slipping? How do you stop snow from getting into your eyes? Would an umbrella work?

My friends and family didn't make things any easier, regularly reminding me of hypothermia, frostbite, and the countless ways you can die during a Canadian winter (polar bears, icy staircases, severe bouts of seasonal affective disorder). My hands already had the habit of turning a sickly green when Melbourne's weather dipped to a meagre ten degrees. "What will happen in minus forty?" my mother wondered aloud, terrified at the prospect.

The biggest shock came from my French tutor, Jean-Claude. Midway through my lesson on plus-que-parfait, I revealed that I was heading to his home province for a university exchange program. I'd be living there for the fall semester, I explained, and would maybe stay through the winter. His eyes widened. He then told me about how, one February morning when he was four, his mother took him out for their daily stroll in Victoriaville. It was cold. It was also the day that his usually diligent mother failed to notice that little Jean-Claude had somehow lost his hat. It took only five minutes for frostbite to set in—leaving Jean-Claude with a right ear that would always remain smaller than his left.

As the last red and yellow leaves fell from their branches, my first Montreal winter was imminent. I tried to ignore the horror stories I'd been inundated with since my arrival, in August. Winter couldn't be that bad. Instead of frozen corpses, I pictured jolly snowmen. I didn't think about the seemingly endless nights; I thought about romantic kisses in the park. In my mind, there were no grey days when the snow made it impossible to see a metre ahead, only visions of perfectly shaped flakes that fell cinematically to the earth.

Luckily, my new friends started giving me advice on how to not only survive the cold but thrive in it. There was Charlotte, who told me about our neglected eleventh finger. During one of our walks to Parc La Fontaine, her phone began to ring. Reaching into her pocket, she swiped to answer the call with her nose. "I hate taking my mittens off" was her response to my dumbfounded expression. Then there was Sara, who encouraged me to eat brie to promote better insulation. Five kilos later, I realized that she was right. There were other tips: take a shot of vodka before outings (it warms you up); befriend your neighbours (they will help push your car when it gets snowed in); and take intermissions on your walks by stepping into oven-heated bagel shops.

Since everything about the season was novel, I could find beauty in even the most unpleasant of physical sensations, whether choking on icy air or getting my eyelashes stuck together.

On a balmy fourteen-degree day in March, while wandering around the foot of Mount Royal in a dress after months spent buried deep in coats, I couldn't help but reflect on my first real winter: the time spent crafting snowballs on my balcony, eating maple taffy in backyards, and being amused by Montreal's starfish children—those innumerable toddlers packed into coral-coloured outfits stiff with padding. I even felt nostalgic for the murky brown street sludge. Winter had been everything I had ever wanted, and yet I will never put myself through it again. The novelty had survived *just* as long as I had. One winter was more than enough.

Remembrance of Poutines Past
Megan Dolski

It was a sweaty night in Stone Town when I sat, sun stroked and hungry, outside my bedroom door. I was squished on a wooden bench with my friends Justin and Riley as we looked out over the ancient city's crooked rooftops. From our perch in that open-air hallway, we watched the sparkling sky as chatter and the squawks from a devastatingly tone-deaf rooster trickled up from the streets below. But our minds had left the bustling East African island for a different one we all knew much better. We were three Montrealers in Zanzibar, thousands of kilometres from Boulevard Saint-Laurent, and laid in front of us were three glorious bowls of steaming poutine.

I had moved to Zanzibar for work nearly a year earlier. My new routine involved seaside sun salutations on the sand instead of attending classes in the Plateau. I'd swapped my favourite run up Côte-Sainte-Catherine for an equally sweaty hill that brought me to the edge of town. I soon learned Swahili well enough to bargain for bananas.

Justin, Riley, and I hadn't all been in the same room for years. A couple of jobs on the West Coast, a stint in Toronto, and a few impromptu adventures had taken them from Montreal too. But an unexpected message from a newly roving Riley and a text from Justin quickly became the beginnings of a plan. A few scattered Skype calls later, the two were at my place in Stone Town, a rented room on the top floor of a house I had found, as one finds all good apartments, through a friend of a friend. We then spent a few days catching up in Bwejuu and Jambiani—fishing villages on the southeast coast of the island. On the drive back to my place, though, we were hit hard by a craving for home. We spiralled off into stories of everyone and everything we missed about Montreal. Then someone got hungry. And, in that moment, the only reasonable response was to make the best Québécois comfort food Zanzibar had ever seen.

As the sun crept downward, we rushed around Stone Town's labyrinthine alleys, gathering supplies before the shops closed for evening prayers. At a tiny storefront, we filled a bag with potatoes from the stash kept out of sight on the floor underneath the counter. We picked up cheese at The Post, the only spot in town with a selection. They didn't have curds, but we made do with a mozzarella-like option that we hoped might get squeaky in the heat. We bought the oil in Lebanon Square. The shop, steps away from my front door, was the closest thing to a dépanneur I had—it opened early, closed late, and sold individual cigarettes and candies. The gravy was easy, waiting in powder form inside my bedroom dresser, scooped from a Canadian care package brought by a friend's visiting father.

Back in my kitchen, frying potatoes and cutting up cheese, we knew that what we were doing was ridiculous. We could have easily gone around the corner for some good greasy chapati mayai. Making poutine seemed silly in the same way as the day before, when we had walked a sprawling beach next to a herd of bumbling cows while immersed in talk of picnics at Parc Jeanne-Mance. It was as absurd as drinking fresh mango juice in front of pristine waters, trying not to overestimate the longevity of the sandbank beneath us, while we craved the lattes and people of Rue Saint-Viateur. We knew it made no sense to be missing those nights spent on Montreal's crooked rooftops, woozily looking out at streets below, while we sat together on another continent, sipping cheap South African wine, staring at the mismatched buildings all around us. But we just couldn't stop.

The three of us had met pulling weekly all-nighters in a newsroom on Boulevard de Maisonneuve. Montreal was a time and a place packed with living, working, and feeling too much. You miss that when you're gone. The bench outside my room was the closest thing we had to a couch, and our conversation was the closest thing we had to home. Six degrees south of the equator, on a tiny island in the Indian Ocean, we ate poutine that night in the same glorious way all Montrealers do—too late, too much, and in the best company.

Cat People
Jason Freure

The alleyway behind my Verdun apartment was a jungle of cat noises all summer. They yelled to be let inside for dinner. They caterwauled as they cruised the streets at midnight. They screeched between parked cars just before dawn, fighting, as I returned from my job at a bar on Crescent.

Four years working the night shift meant I had few chances to see my real friends. On weekends, I dismissed their attempts to set up plans with a quick text, "Sorry, working!" The messages eventually stopped. Night after night, lacking human friendships, I still heard from the cats. Sometimes they even visited my second-floor balcony, hoping for some catnip, before returning to their nightly politics.

One evening in June, I was smoking out there with my girlfriend when she told me that she could hear a cat calling—just one. We waited until our neighbours' windows went dark before we snooped through their yards and traced the source to an old wooden tool shed. From the streetlight, we could see a nose sticking through a rotted-out mouse hole. It belonged to a grey tuxedo—a big one, too; he must have been twenty pounds. We decided to name him Boss.

I came back the next morning and tried to lure Boss through the hole with breakfast. Too fat. I pulled at the door. Locked. Freeing him would mean talking to the neighbours. The teenager who answered the door said that he didn't know where the key to the shed was and his parents were out of town. From the Mario Kart music playing in the background, it was clear he wasn't too interested in helping.

I returned to the shed for the next two days. I fed Boss kibble, scratched him behind his ears. As soon as the food was gone, he started yelling. Come visit me once you're free, I told him. On the third day, I walked out to the shed and it was empty.

Montreal is a city of cats. Most get let out the door on Moving Day, never to find home again. Strays have imprinted themselves on the local consciousness: they skulk out from the streets and into the books of Heather O'Neill and Yves Beauchemin, where they follow drunk eight-year-olds and neglected teens, characters who don't seem particularly capable of living among other people.

When I saw the empty shed, I worried that Boss wasn't a stray after all—that he'd gone home to his owners and I would never see him again. But, that night, he appeared on our balcony, meowing like an alarm clock: "Feed me."

From then on, Boss felt like my cat. I left him breakfast on the balcony every morning. Sometimes he even slept on my lap. "Where did you get so fat? Are you even homeless?" I'd ask, picking him up. He licked his nose and stared at me with dumb, dilated pupils.

By September, I wasn't making much money, and the bar on Crescent looked like it would be going under. Summer had been quiet, and winters always left servers fighting for hours. I regularly came home smelling like beer and Jägermeister and was drinking on the job more than I should've been.

Having Boss around gave me a project, though: after finding some instructions online, I decided to build him a shelter for the coming winter. (We couldn't let him stay with us—he didn't get along with my girlfriend's tabby.) By the time I brought home a big plastic tub and two-centimetre-thick Styrofoam sheets, there was snow on the ground. In need of a box cutter, I went downstairs to our landlords' apartment to see if I could borrow one.

When they answered the door, a ball of grey ran past me and into the alleyway. It was Boss.

I asked them if they knew the cat. My landlords, a couple from Russia, said he'd been staying with them for the past few weeks. I'd been sleeping in after my shifts, so Boss had started creeping through their window and helping himself to their kitchen. They'd quickly given up on trying to kick him out.

I knew I had to let Boss go, but it felt like I was the one getting abandoned. For the next few mornings, I dismissed his meows for a second breakfast with a quick, "Sorry, you're big enough!" The visits eventually stopped.

The bar on Crescent didn't shut down, and I kept coming home at five in the morning. Night after night, I still heard from the cats.

No Woman Is an Island
Deborah Ostrovsky

I was on my way home from buying lunch at La Vieille Europe when I first noticed that the city had changed. As I walked up Saint-Laurent, the street looked like it had been enveloped by a greyish, smoky hue. Maybe the light had simply faded in the slush and grit of another bleak March day. Maybe it was my low blood sugar. Or maybe it was because my marriage was falling apart.

Along the Main, abandoned storefronts declared themselves to be à vendre. I'd grown accustomed to brief incarnations of shops and cafés padlocked just months after opening. But, this time, everything was gone. Even L. Berson & Fils, which had sold Jewish funeral monuments on Saint-Laurent since 1922, was moving away. With a bag of merguez sausages and espresso beans in hand, I stared up at the red-and-grey For Sale sign perched high above piles of granite headstones that awaited their final resting place. I wondered if this was a portent that my relationship was also destined for a graveyard.

My husband and I weren't getting along; trivial

things were adding up. Like when, after over a decade together, he forgot my pathological aversion to birthdays and planned a surprise party for me. It felt like a cruel joke, and I spent most of that night weeping in my bedroom while he entertained our bewildered friends. I was also becoming more of a homebody, scared of air travel, while he chose to work abroad—a fact related to his career ambitions but also an inner need to wander.

Meanwhile, many of our friends' relationships were falling apart. Their negative space was starting to accrete—it felt like only a matter of time before we'd fill it up with our own bad ending. We organized a chalet weekend with another couple who cancelled because they had separated. My daughter had a friend with whom she used to dance to Annie Brocoli songs at daycare. Then one day he was gone: his parents had split up, both moving farther away. While my husband was off in a different time zone, a friend came to pick up our extra bed since her own assets were now divided. *Maybe I'll need that back soon*, I thought, watching her push the mattress into a rental van.

"We are here on this island in the middle of the Pacific in lieu of divorce," Joan Didion wrote in *Life* magazine about a restorative week in Honolulu she spent with her daughter and her husband, the writer John Gregory Dunne. Their plan worked: the marriage lasted until her husband's death, thirty-four years later. The entirety of my marriage has taken place on an island at the confluence of the Saint Lawrence and Ottawa Rivers. In sweat-drenched summers, sharing a bed with someone in an apartment without air conditioning can deal a fatal blow to any relationship. What would have happened had Didion chosen to come here instead?

Our problems ran beyond climate, though. "I'm afraid you married a coureur des bois," my husband's boss (and beloved mentor) once told me, referring to Quebec's early adventurers. We were eating breakfast at a hotel on the northern edge of Germany's Black Forest, where he and my husband were commuting from Montreal—sometimes twice per month—for an engineering project. "He's always on the move," his boss said. I remember my vision going grey then too. I recognized the archetype so well.

My husband and I were about to call it quits when his beloved boss, married longer than anyone I knew, died. On a muggy, sunny August morning, we made our way up Mount Royal to the cemetery. The gravestone came from L. Berson & Fils's new iteration.

I stood at the graveside, and my blurry grey vision went away. *This is how things will end*, I thought. The funeral took place on one of the brightest days I can remember—nature's cruel way of asserting its joyful will amid a crowd of mourners. As we drove down the mountain, things appeared gilt edged. My husband announced that he had cancelled a few upcoming trips. We talked about flying to Honolulu.

Unlike Didion and her husband, we never made it to the Pacific. Instead, we ended up at a Cistercian abbey in Saint-Jean-de-Matha, just an hour away. Eschewing artisanal cheeses and rosaries in the gift shop, we picked up a self-help book called *Le couple* with Gustav Klimt's *The Kiss* on the cover.

We haven't finished the book. We probably never will. But we got off the island, and that was good enough.

A Site for Soirées
Hélène Bauer

"To a place where you would have never met otherwise," said Emory, raising his glass. Around the table, twelve of us joined the host's toast as a chef on his day off from Maison Publique emerged from the kitchen with a plate of steaming cauliflower.

I joined Emory and eleven other early-twenties diners for a new Monday night tradition. Though we were a typical collection of students and young graduates, we were not in a typical Mile End student apartment—no collection of beer bottles, no ashtray full of cigarette butts. Rather, it featured antique furniture and a long dark oak table, which, admittedly, had been used to play beer pong. We all made an effort to dress a little more chic than usual, as if rising to meet the spirit of the house.

The house, at 440 Rue Bonsecours, is in the heart of Old Montreal. Save for a tiny plaque, nothing about the building indicates that it is a special place. But, in this house, Louis-Joseph Papineau started a francophone revolution. There wasn't room for two languages in Papineau's Montreal, and to this day, the aftermath of his uproar continues to echo throughout the city. At this party, francophones and anglophones blended together, switching from one language to the other. Papineau would have hated it.

Louis-Joseph Papineau was the leader of the mid-nineteenth-century Patriote movement in Lower Canada. The French Canadian nationalist devoted his life to fighting the British occupation of Montreal. Known locally as both a hero and a conspirator, Papineau was one of the first to defend the importance of French culture in the city.

Between 1819 and 1837, Papineau and his wife had climbed the same staircase I used to reach the top-floor apartment that was now my friends' home. It was here that Papineau drafted the ninety-two resolutions of 1834: a long list of political demands for the British-governed colony, including the reinstatement of the French as head of government and French as the leading language in Montreal. While the government of Lower Canada adopted these resolutions, they were later rejected by the British government.

In Montreal, Papineau's efforts were met with uproar by anglophones. On November 6, 1837, a loyalist group called the Doric Club attacked Maison

Papineau: the bloody protest rang in the start of many armed confrontations between the two sides. The battles lasted two years, during which Montreal fell under military control, and ended only when Lower and Upper Canada were forcibly united as one political entity under the Act of Union, in 1840. Papineau, however, wasn't around to witness the end of his rebellion: in 1839, after a warrant had been issued for his arrest, he fled first to New York and then to France.

In Papineau's time, his home on Bonsecours was in the heart of the city. After he left, the neighbourhood slid into decrepitude as families moved closer to Mount Royal and businesses moved to Sainte-Catherine and Saint-Laurent. By the 1990s, after decades of lying fallow, what is now called Old Montreal was aided by renewal efforts in recovering most of its old-world charm—but not much of its glory.

Fast track 176 years from Papineau's flight to summer 2015. Emory, along with two friends, moved into the old home. While the Government of Canada bought the building in 1982 and Parks Canada began to transform it into a site commemorating Papineau, Emory was able to take over his grandmother's lease of the attic apartment. Inspired by Papineau, the three decided to host Monday-night dinners. They select a diverse guest list, asking each diner to cover food and drinks and bring their best conversation.

There's no doubt that hidden between the cracks of each hardwood floor panel and recessed window are countless secrets that helped forge Montreal's identity. Empowered by this almost tangible force, the boys have transformed the home into a modern-day salon: an incubator where graffiti artists, startup entrepreneurs, chefs, and DJs cross paths.

In the presence of Papineau's ghost, we eat roast beef and digress in both national languages. As the conversation with my neighbour starts to fade, I listen in on a Québécois bartender wearing oversized glasses explaining in English why she believes Prague is the new Berlin.

In this home where Papineau crafted a French rebellion, we're rekindling that revolutionary spirit not by breaking away from the other but by bridging the cultural gap that plagued him.

The Still Waters of the Saint Lawrence
Maija Kappler

When I was fourteen, I skinned my knee roller-blading. It was summertime, and I was eager to get down to the lakeshore near my house in Lachine, a suburb along the southern edge of the island of Montreal. I had successfully navigated my pothole-laden street only to tumble as soon as I reached the smooth, paved bike lane that flanks the shore.

Even from the ground, everything looked as calm as ever. A few tall pine trees swayed in the wind; the water from Lac Saint-Louis lapped placidly against the rocks on the shoreline. I remember being surprised at how many different shades of red erupted from the wound on my leg. The worst part, though, was that I had ruined my favourite jeans: one clean rip across the left knee.

For Proust, eating a madeleine was enough to be transported back to a different time and place, but some memories you can't access from a distance. I forgot about my bloodied knee until I was back in the exact spot where it happened. Every time I go back to the lakeshore, something like that will resurface: too small to carry around in my real life, not small enough to disappear entirely. A sound, a smell, the twisty feeling I got in my stomach when I fought with my best friends in grade five. Out of nowhere, I can recall the ideas I had as a child about who I was going to be, like something cast away long ago that comes bobbing back through the water, improbably preserved.

Lachine is boring. The small suburb is nestled uncomfortably between the anglophone heterogeneity of the West Island and the hip metro-accessible boroughs of Verdun and Notre-Dame-de-Grâce. I moved out of my parents' house as soon as I could afford to. *It's not really a place worth knowing about*, I explain apologetically to people in Toronto who ask what part of Montreal I'm from. *The metro doesn't even go out there.*

But the lakeshore has always been special. A few decades ago, before I was born, Lachine began buying up and demolishing old buildings along its waterfront. It started in the fifties, when the passage of new laws forbade anything new from being built on the south side of Boulevard Saint-Joseph and several old buildings in the borough's industrial east end were torn down. But the bulk of the work was done in the 1970s, under mayor Guy Descary, who wanted more parks for the city's residents. One of the last houses to go, an elegant two-storey with a private tennis court, was torn down in the late nineties; its stained-glass windows were sold off one by one. Now, anyone can walk along the water on paths that stretch from Lachine's western border with Dorval all the way into Old Montreal.

Unlike the rest of Lachine, the lakeshore is beautiful enough to draw visitors. It's comfortingly vast, and the sky is never quite as vivid anywhere else in the city. My friends and I played there as kids, and as teenagers, we snuck beers out of the fridge and drank them at a spot where the shore juts out toward the water. We shared secrets in what used to be someone's backyard, creating private memories in a newly public space.

The last time I was home, I met up with two old friends for a walk by the lake. We took the path that winds along the waterfront, past the houses where we grew up, past palatial homes and modest apartment blocks. Someone had set up a drum kit dangerously close to the shoreline, the drummer mostly obscured by tall reeds. Cyclists whizzed by. We passed the spot where I skinned my knee at fourteen, where you can see a tiny uninhabited island just off the shore, its tangled mess of green branches bound up, in my memory, with a pair of torn jeans.

We'd been out only a few minutes when we ran into some girls we knew, a pair of twins. They had been our best friends in elementary school and then, later on, the sworn enemies of another friend. Now they're just people we knew when we were young. They were stretched out on a big blue blanket, shoes off, drinking cans of Palm Bay. We performed a ritualistic catch-up dance: *Oh, you're getting married? Congratulations! What's he like? I'm living in Toronto. It's great, but there's something about home, you know?*

While we talked about how much things had changed, the sound of the water against the rocks reminded us that nothing had, not really.

Ollies in Outremont
Kyle Carney

One weekday afternoon in August 1999, when I was a high school student, my friend Akber and I were skateboarding in Place de la Paix, a then-unofficial skate park in downtown Montreal. Two police officers arrived soundlessly on bikes. We expected to receive a warning since we hadn't been there long and the park was quiet that day—we were bothering no one. Citing a noise complaint, they took our IDs and issued us tickets. We were each fined $65 for disturbing the peace.

We were shocked. The black granite ledges that edged Place de la Paix were too tall to be steps, too short to be benches; like so much of Montreal's terrain and architecture, they seemed made for us. My friends and I skirted the pavement in thunderous packs, threading the traffic of Sainte-Catherine or swerving between tourists at city hall.

We hurled our bodies over the stairways of the Palais de justice, threw ourselves against the banked walls of the Stade olympique. While our parents were at work, we swirled around drained fountains and glided across waxed curbs. Church steeples and tarnished statues loomed above our kickflips. In Chinatown and the Old Port, we tick-tacked along cobblestone and brick alleyways. At Square Victoria, we gleamed the cube, then we shredded the gnar of Westmount hills. Through blissful manoeuvres and brutal injuries, we came to worship the city and its streets.

In many ways, we were descendants of *The Devil's Toy*, a fifteen-minute skate flick directed by Claude Jutra (whose legacy was marred by multiple child-abuse accusations that emerged after he died) and originally released as *Rouli-roulant* in 1966. In the opening scene, the Montreal cityscape is briefly captured in black and white, only a year before Expo 67 and the completion of the ever-troublesome Turcot Interchange. The tongue-in-cheek short satirically portrays skateboarders as public enemies.

The skaters, boys and girls dressed in preppy Sunday clothes, chug from glass bottles of milk. Their movements are primitive, their boards narrow, their wheels made of clay. They cruise along park pathways and navigate narrow corners. Jazz plays listlessly in the background. Despite the narrator's stern warnings, the skaters seem absolutely harmless.

But it's not long before the police arrive. The kids toss their boards into bushes and scatter away on foot. The coppers manage to trap the luckless, who suffer confiscation. With a hint of an Irish accent, one of the policemen says, "You're not allowed to use these things."

The Devil's Toy, ostensibly a spoof, is not far off the mark when it comes to the relationship between skateboarders and the law. As a teen, I was forever fielding the inquiries of police officers, security guards, schoolteachers, and concerned citizens. I was chased down and chastised, forced to conceal what I was doing and, like the milk-chugging teens of *Rouli-roulant*, to jettison my beloved board. I once lost a deck for several days after trying to escape an angry custodian and had to crawl through a dense thicket to find it.

In the closing scenes of *Rouli-roulant*, everyone regroups for a skate session atop a windswept hill. Thirty-three years later, I was similarly undeterred. Within moments of getting my ticket in Place de la Paix, I was back on my board.

Skateboarding is a sport for the young. An easily separated shoulder forced me to quit ten years ago, and I don't even own a board anymore—I bestowed my last deck upon my nephews, who have no use for it. Nevertheless, skating haunts my daydreams. I remember the way Montreal revealed itself to me in new and fascinating ways. We'd happen upon a hidden ledge, or a bump would manifest in the pavement. I recall, with fondness, the myriad treasures of Lachine's industrial sector, the ramped planters of Avenue McGill College, the gaps and curved barriers of construction sites. The poetry of a tailslide or a wallride, the illusionism of a hardflip. The concrete landscape was transformed by my trickery, and my mundane surroundings turned into something more lyrical.

There's a skate park down the street from my apartment. Several times a day, I can hear the unmistakable growl of wheels hitting concrete, the sound of the next generation of skaters discovering Montreal anew. I still look at the city streets— glimpsing an overturned shopping cart or a paved slope—with the same wild fascination, imagining the possibilities.

You Want to Travel with Him
Erica Ruth Kelly

It was hard to breathe in front of the fire. As a five-alarm blaze ravaged the abandoned R. S. Muir & Co. building at Parc and Milton, large plumes of smoke towered over the surrounding area, turning the sky grey. Donald Trump had recently won the US presidential election, and I was afraid to exhale. CTV News later reported that the fire department had realized the building could not be saved—the only way to gain control of the fire was to tear it down.

Drifting snow fell softly as the firefighters pressed on. It disappeared on contact, touching the empty winding sidewalks and Victorian architecture of the McGill ghetto. I warmed myself by walking to Leonard Cohen's makeshift memorial site, outside his home on Rue Vallières, near Saint-Laurent, just over ten blocks away. Our hometown hero had been dead a little over two weeks.

I first read Leonard Cohen's poetry over twenty years ago, in the first edition of *15 Canadian Poets*, an unwittingly ironic gift from my god-fearing Irish-Catholic grandmother.

"Perhaps a mind will open in this world / perhaps a heart will catch rain," he wrote in "Style," a poem that made the world seem magical. "Nothing will heal and nothing will freeze / but perhaps a heart will catch rain." I loved him immediately. He opened up parts of my brain and body I didn't know existed. He made everything seem volatile, full of hope and despair and peace and suffering, simultaneously possible and impossible. He created nihilist dreamers and romantic disciples set on revolution, teaching us that the most we could ever hope for was to delight in a state of gentle, violent becoming. If you were lucky, maybe you could thrive there. All you needed were the right words. After discovering Cohen, I began to carry a pen everywhere I went.

"Everyone who loves him goes through that phase," Jason said a few hours before I walked by the fire. "The phase where you really, really love him." Jason was one of my favourite English professors at Concordia and one of my favourite poets too. He and I had often talked about Cohen over the years. I talked about how indebted I felt to him but also about how much he owed poets like us: no writer from Montreal can avoid comparison. We don't stand on the shoulders of a giant so much as we stand in his shadow.

Cohen's shadow followed me as I wound my way through the city, relying on muscle memory. I had left Montreal for Toronto a few years earlier, and this was my first visit since his death. I made my way from Jason's office at De Maisonneuve and Mackay through the somewhat solemn dimly lit McGill campus, where Cohen had gone to school. I wondered how my life would've been different had I chosen to go there instead of Concordia. I walked by The Word bookstore on Milton, where I used to take dates—where Cohen smiled down at me from the *Let Us Compare Mythologies* poster that hung on the store's wall. I walked up past the fiery R. S. Muir & Co. onto the Plateau and into the neighbourhood that will forever be associated with Cohen.

His house was on the southern edge of Parc du Portugal, a small park dedicated to Montreal's Portuguese community. Cohen would have seen the small gazebo across the street every time he opened his front door, against which the city's love and grief were now laid: palpable, tangible, itemized. Rows of dying bouquets. Boxes of tea and oranges, a nod to "Suzanne." One stale bagel—possibly from Bagel Etc., which Cohen was known to frequent—left untouched by respectful pigeons.

After a parked car drove off, no one remained in front of the house. The street was quiet. Despite having developed relationships based on my love for Cohen, I wanted to be alone when I paid my respects and said goodbye. I decided to add a note to the many already scattered around the memorial. But what could I possibly say? Could it ever be as good as what he might write for someone he had lost? I fumbled through my bag. My hand felt around again. And again. I didn't have a pen. Even if the right words had come to me, I had no way to write them. I smiled to myself as my shoulders dropped, humbled and relieved.

Was the fire out yet? I didn't know. But I felt like I could finally breathe.

A Schwartz's in Paris
Katie Sehl

North of the Arc de Triomphe's starbursting giratoire, in the tourist-free seventeenth arrondissement of Paris, I caught sight of a beacon from back home. The sign promised to satiate my North American taste for meat with a cut of beef far more familiar than the Parisian penchant for steak tartare and tripe: it was Schwartz's cherry-red logo, signature swoosh and all.

Those who were initiated at the Hebrew delicatessen on the Main—the once Jewish-settled artery that fed working class immigrants and buffered Montreal's English and French solitudes with shops and factories—know that there is a certain level of devotion one must bring to the table. The sandwich is to be eaten with a Cott Black Cherry soda, a side of fries, and a single kosher dill pickle, all served on separate plates. If you must ask your server to hold the yellow mustard, you won't be charged a rule-breaking fee as is threatened at Wilensky's Light Lunch on Fairmount, but you'll get a suspicious glare and a grunt from the sandwich maker forced to work against his muscle-memory mustard-swiping rhythm. And, when asked how you'd like your sandwich, the only correct response is "medium fat."

In Paris, after ordering, I sat ready for the question to be asked, but my waiter was already on his way back to the kitchen. Over my shoulder, another waiter asked a patron how they'd like their Yankee Burger. "Saignant." When my waiter returned with the Dr. Pepper I'd settled for in lieu of a cherry soda, I asked if the establishment and its two sister locations in Paris were affiliated with the Montreal institution. "Non," he huffed.

Burgers, currently on trend in Paris, take up the first page of doppelgänger Schwartz's menu. In another strange inversion, English precedes French and is even a few font points larger. Smoked meat— the ambiguously named pièce de resistance of the original Schwartz's sandwich—is nowhere to be found on the Paris menu, and neither is viande fumée. Instead, page two offers options for smoked meat's New York cousin: pastrami.

Both deli meats hail from a tradition brought to the New World in the early nineteenth century by Jewish Romanian immigrants, but their development hit a fork in the road thanks, in part, to British imperialism in Canada. In the United

States, pastrami is made with navel, a dense and fatty cut from near the belly. North of the border, British butchery standards made navel harder to come by, making brisket—a stringier cut from the forequarters—the standard for smoked meat. Schwartz's secret spice mix, coupled with an eight-decade buildup of schmutz (the fat and spices that have accumulated on the smokehouse's brick walls), add essential flavour to their sandwich and partially explain why the Montreal institution hasn't franchised. Schwartz's schmutz wasn't built in a day.

Schwartz's Montreal nearly lost its possessive apostrophe, an Anglo attribution outlawed chez nous when the French Language Office came knocking in 1996. The name, apostrophe and all, is under copyright protection in North America but not in France, which is how the French franchise gets away with its knock-off branding. In Paris, the punctuation mark is deliberately exotic, casually dotting signs around the city.

The unaffiliated Parisian pastrami comes in three sandwich varieties: The Best Hot Pastrami Sandwich, The Reuben, and The Very Best Hot Pastrami Sandwich. The Best offers hot pastrami topped with barbecue sauce; The Reuben, hot pastrami with coleslaw, onion, and melted Emmenthal;

and The Very Best, hot veal pastrami with honey mustard. As a rule-following devotee of Schwartz's Montreal, I opted for the latter because it felt closest to the original.

As I sipped my Dr. Pepper and waited, I looked to the walls for reassurance. At home, I'd find a newspaper-cut pantheon of Montreal idols: Céline Dion, Mordecai Richler, and retired Habs players offering B-list blessings over bifteck rituals. Instead, I found black-and-white photos of the Guggenheim and the Chrysler Building and advertisements for Budweiser beer and Francis Ford Coppola wines. Lording over it all, Uncle Sam pointed down defiantly at the dining area, reserving the right to refuse service to anyone—"This includes YOU." I began to indulge in a favourite Canadian pastime: taking quiet offence, but also pride, over the French American repackaging of our very best.

It wasn't the taste of home I came for, but I relished the feeling—and the sandwich—nonetheless. I threw out the rulebook. "Garçon," I called as I finished my Dr. Pepper. "I'll take a glass of Coppola Rosso California Blend." Vive la différence.

Leaf Thief
Will Keats-Osborn

Early last year, while attending a memorial for my grandmother in Gridley, California, I stole a plant from my cousin's garden. The cousin was hosting us in her sprawling farmhouse bungalow sheltered by rows of walnut trees. In the carefully tended garden that encircled the house, birds sang as they flitted between the branches of a giant magnolia; a potato vine scaling the trellis above the patio was flush with white flowers. The root of the Central Valley's fecundity—the warm, warm sun—bathed everything in light.

The plant I took was a silver squill, a tiny onion-like bulb with a spray of pewter-coloured leaves emerging from its top. A silver squill yields new bulbs as its outer layers of skin peel away until, over time, a teeming assembly of them gathers; a cluster of the plants had colonized a wok-shaped pot on my cousin's patio. I ripped out a bulb without asking and squirrelled it away in my jacket pocket, intent on smuggling it back to Canada and making it mine.

I once copped an aloe pup from a municipal garden. I've plucked a palmful of sedums from a living wall. The elephant bush sitting on the window ledge in my kitchen came from the courtyard of a model home. These thefts are a compulsion that compounds the sin of keeping plants inside: plants from the deserts and tropics of the world, like the South African squill, don't want to live indoors, least of all in Montreal. But people like me keep bringing them here for our own benefit, to lift us up when winter's eternal darkness drags us down. The stolen ones have the virtue of being free.

If you're conscientious about your plants, the cost comes later, when the moral hazard of plant ownership starts to weigh on you. Like a caged songbird, a houseplant improves your life by surrendering much of its own. Whatever conditions made a plant's original niche home are now yours to worry about, and the penalty of negligence is death. There are no earthworms mixing the soil, no microbes fixing nitrogen in the leaf litter, no predators grazing on parasites, no rainfall dampening the earth. However hard an indoor gardener tries to fill all these roles at once, it's impossible to replace the sun as it lolls behind banks of snow-laden clouds. It's all you can do to crowd your houseplants against a window and watch helplessly as a dull beam sweeps across your apartment like a searchlight, finding each languid plant for only a moment.

For me, the thought of this cost ebbs whenever I exit the metro at Kiosque Mont-Royal in the summertime or linger in a florist's stall at Marché Jean-Talon. (Plants! So many plants!) The thought of the anemic winter sun didn't cross my mind for the two long days the squill sat in my pocket as I wandered through the walnut groves and spent time with my family in Gridley. Pests were a distant notion as I sweated in the customs line, wondering which pockets they would check if they pulled me aside for a special screening.

It was only at home, once I'd nestled the squill in some fresh potting soil, that the worry set in. The thin stalk of buds that adorned the plant when I plucked it bloomed soon after I arrived—tiny fairy bells hung with bright-yellow stamens on purple filaments. As it flowered, though, the bulb shrivelled down to the size and shape of a raisin, and from tip to base, each of its three leaves dried up, one by one. Clearly, I thought, the beleaguered pup was directing what remained of its life force at a desperate effort to sow some seeds before it became a casualty of my self-indulgence.

I needed the squill as a salve for my dreary

moods. A tonic for my impatience. A cure for the wishful thinking each early thaw inspires, repeatedly nudging the prospect of spring further into the future.

After two suspenseful weeks—when the flowers were wilted and lifeless—the squill saved me as it saved itself. The final leaf was half gone when a new curl of green poked out from the bulb, now swelling with life. Such a relief! Because what kind of person rends a plant from its sunny California garden and brings it to a third-floor walk-up in Little Italy only to watch over it as it dies? I may steal plants, but I'm not depraved. I simply need them to live.

On the Lam
Ziya Jones

When the weather is warm, Parc du Pélican—a midsize semi-suburban park flanked by apartment buildings in Rosemont–La Petite-Patrie—fills with locals. Young families swim in the pool; teenagers stake out the bleachers, the smell of weed carrying on the air along with their laughter. But, today, a drizzly day in July, the rain is keeping people away. Which is why there's almost no one around to see me chasing down the ewe.

A hulking mass of white wool with black spots, the fugitive is one of a flock of ten. She and her pen mates—five other ewes and four lambs—were brought in from a farm in the Laurentians: Montreal will host them from June to August. As part of an urban agriculture project, they'll help mow the lawns in three Rosemont parks and awaken city dwellers to the benefits of sustainable farming. A few months ago, I saw an open callout for apprentice shepherds and immediately signed up, figuring I'd catch on quickly. No one told me about the sprinting.

This isn't the escaped sheep's first brush with trouble. She acts out so often that, by the end of the summer, program organizers will have bitterly nicknamed her "Merguez." This afternoon, her rebellion is fuelled by dissatisfaction. Like us, sheep are prone to believing that whatever is slightly out of reach must be better than what's within their grasp. Dissatisfied with the pen's soggy grass, Merguez hops the plastic fence and takes off running. Her lumbering dash lasts for about twenty metres before I'm able to outpace her and block her path, stretching my arms and doing my best impression of a linebacker. Merguez skids and turns to avoid me, then heads back toward the pen. When she gets there, I give her a little push, and she leaps back inside—but not before another ewe realizes how much fun she's been missing and takes off on her own great escape.

This rainy morning, I learn that the stereotypes we're taught about sheep don't hold up: they may be instinctual followers, but they are surprisingly difficult to control.

The summer I lord over the sheep, anxiety lords over me. I've just ended a relationship with a man I loved deeply for teaching me that I deserved to feel safe. Eventually, safety wasn't enough, and I left. But now I'm regretful and untethered.

In September, I'll fly across the continent with my best friend to support him after he has major surgery. For a time, he won't be able to sit up, stand, brush his teeth, or use the bathroom without help. I'll manage his medication, make his meals, be his arms, legs, and hands. I'm not ready.

On weekends, I take advantage of Montreal's ability to make a person feel lost. The sweaty dance floor at Bar Le Ritz PDB and the smoke-filled sidewalks lining Saint-Laurent hum with enough fear and desire to distract me from my own. I stay out late, wake with the sun, then lie in bed shaking with dread until it's time to get it together and report for my volunteer shepherding shift.

Whenever I'm with the sheep, the worry reel slows, replaced by the immediate need to keep them from accidentally bolting into the road. Eventually, many of them will likely become food, as animals raised on their farm often do—for now, though, they have no idea about their fate. For the sheep, there's only the present moment. And, for the few hours a week I spend with them, we're grounded by the same things: the smell of the hay, the coolness of the rain, the sound of constant bleating.

By August, we've moved the sheep to their final Rosemont location: Parc Beaubien, a large rectangular green space two kilometres north of Pélican. Here, we don't bother with the pen—after weeks of futile corralling, we let the animals wander free, only intervening if a ewe strays too far from the herd or too close to the road. Delighted children zigzag through the field alongside the sheep, and everyone—yuppie dog walkers, cellphone-wielding teens, bar-bound francophone men—stops to take a look. Even in Montreal, an island that sometimes feels more like a fun fair than a functioning city, the appearance of a flock of sheep invites pause.

One sunny afternoon, I spot a ewe munching on a long vine protruding through a chain-link fence from someone's yard, playing arborist when she should be playing lawnmower. I consider shooing her, but I know she'll be back the second I turn away. Instead, I exhale and watch her as she chews, vacant and peaceful. Today, pleasure reigns over order. And why not? There's so little we can control in this life. Sometimes all we can do is try our best to herd one another through.

Notre Dame D'Espace
Michelle Deines

My sister's train was late. It was supposed to arrive at Montreal Central Station at seven, and it was now twenty past. It was 1996, and no one had cellphones. All I had to go by was the information posted on the massive platform display hanging over the middle of the cavernous concourse, which declared that my sister's train was À l'heure/ On Time.

My God, I was tired—a profound, deep-in-the-bones exhaustion. My head ached. My eyes hurt. My limbs felt heavy. I leaned my forehead against the wall, the coolness of the polished granite soothing in the humid May evening. The station was quiet, and I could have fallen asleep right there.

I was reeling from the year I'd just finished at the University of Victoria: more than a full-time course load, long nights working on theatre productions, longer nights with my first boyfriend, and on weekend mornings, at seven o'clock, working as a caregiver for a man I'll call Andrew. I was twenty. What did I know? I kept that schedule up for eight months. I didn't realize how drained I had become until I arrived in Montreal that spring.

I'd gone to Montreal to accompany Andrew at his brother's wedding. I'd been there less than a week when Andrew's mother—who was also my boss—pulled me into the office of their enormous suburban home.

"You know," she said, "your shirt is missing buttons."

I did know. It was my favourite, a green flannel. It was the nineties.

"Andrew really likes you, but . . ."

I spent that evening weeping into the phone. I felt like I had been betrayed and abandoned because my employer just didn't like me. It was a new feeling: I'd never been fired before. I felt like a failure.

My father insisted I fly home immediately. I had one friend in Montreal, though, Colleen, who invited me to stay with her in Notre-Dame-de-Grâce, a residential neighbourhood west of downtown.

The smart thing to do, I knew, was to go home. But it suddenly occurred to me what getting fired, as demoralizing as it was, really meant. I looked at my Day-Timer. I'd written "Montreal" on the date of my arrival and drawn an arrow across the otherwise blank week.

"I'll come tomorrow," I told Colleen.

The next day, I knocked on the door of her big brick walk-up on Décarie, a quiet boulevard of apartment buildings and small community centres. "Stay as long as you want," she said. She left shortly afterward for her own summer job.

I had an apartment to myself, barely any money, and no one to talk to—my French was deplorable. It was glorious. I rescheduled my flight, extending my trip by two weeks.

I spent much of my time going for walks. I window-shopped along Monkland, peeked into bagel shops and cafés on Sherbrooke, and meandered through residential streets twisting past small playgrounds and vacant lots. When I felt like splurging, I counted out my nickels and dimes, took the bus downtown, and wandered past second-hand shops on Saint-Laurent and baseball and soccer games in Parc Jeanne-Mance. Joggers huffed down the sidewalks; drivers swore at one another in the street. The air smelled like sap and smoke, the terrasses were full, and the city seemed delighted that summer—humid, stifling—had finally begun. I slept heavily every night, windows open to the sounds of the city.

Finally ready for company, I invited my sister, who lived in Toronto, to come up for a weekend.

But, now, I was starting to worry that something had gone wrong with her train. I shifted in my chair, my legs sticking to the plastic.

Then the display began to flash: Arrivé. I stood to watch the passengers emerge, waiting until they'd all come and gone. My sister wasn't among them. I wanted to cry. Had she missed her train? I checked my watch. It was now seven forty-five and I had no way of—wait. I looked at my watch again. The date read Thursday. My sister was arriving on Friday.

Of course I had come to the train station a day early: I hadn't looked at a calendar, much less set an alarm, in days. Montreal's haziness was finally starting to get under my skin. Back home, I collapsed into bed. A breeze kicked up scents through my window: cut grass, car exhaust, cigarettes. My sister would arrive at Central Station, and I would be there, just a little more rested, the next day.

Home Ice
Carly Rosalie Vandergriendt

As I pulled up to my first apartment in Montreal, my boyfriend appeared on the second-
storey balcony, waving, as if on cue. I was in my
early twenties, and my parents, in a show of sup-
portiveness, had spent Labour Day ferrying me
east along the 401, all the way from my hometown
in southern Ontario to a postwar sixplex in La
Petite-Patrie.

I had moved for love, and my boyfriend, Simon-
Pierre, was ready to return the favour by helping me
lug my stuff up the stairs—including a black canvas
wheelie bag spacious enough to conceal a body.

"What's this?" he asked, unzipping it in our
foyer. He peered at its contents: padded shorts, a
neck guard, a sweat-stained pelvic protector.

"I play hockey," I said. We'd met while tree-
planting, and some details from our everyday lives
had never surfaced.

How's this for a Canadian cliché? My family
celebrates Christmas by renting out an ice rink to
play pickup hockey. Five-year-olds play alongside

fifty-five-year-olds, women among men. We keep score. An ex–figure skater, I swapped my leotards for a jersey at thirteen; at my first hockey practice, I kept rolling off the rounded toe of my new skates. My new black skates—how transgressive. I played in an all-girls minor league until university, when I joined a coed intramural league. Over the years, hockey became more than just something I did; it became part of my identity. Figure skating had been all poise, but hockey was primal.

Those first few months in Montreal, I asked around about a women's league. But Simon-Pierre, who'd never brandished a stick in his life, was part of an artsy coterie that turned up scant leads. As fall gave way to my first Montreal winter, I took solitary walks near my new apartment. One day, about a block away, I came upon an outdoor rink in a park and paused to watch the late-afternoon melee.

Players in their late teens and twenties whipped around the ice, steam emanating from their exposed cheeks. Occasionally, one of them would let out a grunt—a truncated battle cry. The grind of their blades and the clatter of their sticks reminded me of my childhood, of evenings spent in the artificial deep freeze of the arena. But there was one difference: they were all men. I thought about coming back with my skates, but as I turned toward home, I knew I wouldn't.

I passed that rink often, but I never saw another woman there. It was Les Boys—not exactly shocking, but coupled with the lack of a women's league, it made me curious. Could a province that had produced greats like Manon Rhéaume, Kim St-Pierre, and Caroline Ouellette actually not be such a great place to be a hockeyeuse?

Simon-Pierre and I were in his car on our way to a holiday dinner when I heard an interview on Radio-Canada with a journalist named Lynda Baril, who'd just written a book on the history of women's hockey in Quebec. A century ago, she explained, the province's first female players were Anglo-Saxons. The Catholic Church actually forbade French Canadian women from playing hockey, which it deemed unfeminine. Was that the legacy I was noticing at my local patinoire?

It bothered me that I couldn't bring myself to just join the game. I was a strong, scrappy skater. I suspected that the problem was my newly acquired fish-out-of-water status. I was the odd one out, the anglophone among Simon-Pierre's friends and family. Perhaps I didn't want to be the odd one out on the ice too.

A few years later, when my parents gave Simon-Pierre a pair of hockey skates for Christmas, things changed—he wanted to play too. In January, we met some friends at the outdoor rink, throwing our sticks down at centre ice along with the others. A scruffy-faced guy in a plaid jacket sorted the sticks into two piles.

Then the puck dropped, and my face prickled with the cold air as I picked up speed and followed it deep into the corner. Someone was behind me in a second, digging at my skates. An elbow pressed into my back as I flicked the puck up the boards. The game moved fast, flipping from one end of the small rink to the other in the blink of an eye. Without equipment, it was rough, but I didn't mind. In every tussle, I could feel how deeply I'd missed playing. If the men on the ice cared that I was a woman, I didn't notice—because, for that brief game, I forgot too.

The Rides of March
andrea bennett

"My bike is fricked," my friend Ziya texted me. It was mid-March 2016, nearly the end of my first Montreal winter. Overwhelming piles of snow had finally given way to gravel-specked islets, a combination of snow and dirt I learned had been portmanteaued as "snirt." The trees, denuded, had not yet begun to bud. I was about to start a new job as a bike mechanic.

Ziya's bike—a rusty orange single-speed city cruiser—was, indeed, fricked. They'd pulled it out of storage for a spring ride and left it locked about ten metres from the front door of their apartment building, resting against the wall of an elementary school. Later, we surveyed the damage: a snowplow had hit the pedals and part of the frame, mangling both.

Later that March, I snapped a photo of a green mountain bike, prone on the ground, missing its rear wheel. It had been locked to a post, which had also been uprooted. The fork had snapped clean off the frame. The following February, near McGill,

I caught another good one: a red mountain bike with white handlebars and a foreshortened front end—chained to a pole with its nose sticking out onto the sidewalk flanking Avenue des Pins, it had been chastened for its impertinence.

I'd begun to collect the bikes as if they were Pokémon. "Just a flesh wound!" I wrote on Instagram, excited to find a good specimen. Winter is tough in Montreal, but the early spring—what I came to think of as dead-stick season, when the snow is gone and dirt and dog shit have replaced it—is even worse. I'm not proud to admit it, but the city's absurdly mangled bikes propelled me through the dregs of March and April until the leaves and flowers finally began to emerge in May.

Every October, red and yellow snow markers begin sprouting around the driveways, bushes, and retaining walls of Montreal. Standing waist- or sometimes even shoulder-high, they signal caution to the sidewalk plows. But every borough contracts its own snow-removal services, some companies aren't as scrupulous as others, and much of the property we wish to remain unmangled is transient and unmarkable: bikes, cars, and strollers too large and bulky to store inside one's cramped two-bedroom walk-up.

In January 2017, one Montrealer recorded a video of a plow fishtailing wildly down his street; Global News aired it alongside another video of a plow running down a bike and a city signpost, seemingly on purpose. Pavages d'Amour (ironically, "pavings of love"), the contractor responsible for the damage, was fined $150,000 by the city and then had its lucrative contract cancelled. Though stats aren't available on plow-damaged property in Montreal, the phenomenon is common enough that one CBC article refers to the snowplow as "the bike's natural predator." As municipal politics writ small, the plow-mangled bikes are kind of funny, kind of crooked, kind of sad; collecting and disseminating their images allowed me to feel like a Montrealer or at least a chronicler of a tiny corner of the city's stories.

In late February 2018, with climate change creating pockets of warmth even within Montreal's heady winters, I came across a red vélo sport mixte. Its front wheel had been plow-caught and twisted, now lying perpendicular to the frame. "A fork in the road," I captioned the pic I posted, newly a parent and ready to reach for the lowest-hanging dad joke. In March, I posted a wonky Supercycle and applied for a job across the country, in Vancouver, where my partner's mom and sister live.

When I got the job, I cried. Vancouver was the city we'd left to move to Montreal in the first place, and we had deeply missed its mountains and oceans and overwhelmingly large trees. But I now loved Montreal too.

As we packed, it felt like I had unfinished business—I would no longer be the unasked-for chronicler of Montreal's orphaned bicycles, with their tacoed wheels and bent derailleurs. I would no longer be yearning for the briny West Coast air; instead, I'd be yearning for the first city that had come to feel like home.

Melting Pot
Fionn Adamian

No doubt I was making a mess of things. It was half an hour until close on my first dish-washing shift at a Rosemont smokehouse, and the pots, the vats, the pans all piled up reproachfully in the sink, covered with stubborn smears of Carolina barbecue and Québécois gravy. As I hunched over, scrubbing, the odd bead of sweat dripping onto the sponge, I noticed a goopy yellow liquid with strands of green oozing up from the drain; judging by the colour, a mixture of mac 'n' cheese and spinach had clogged the sink. I was jerkily thrusting the plunger when suddenly the chef turned to me and shouted a question.

I was agog, as if cold-called in lecture; I was light-headed. It was July, at the height of the heat wave, temperatures cresting at forty degrees with the humidity. Was it the heat? Or did I just not speak enough French?

"Découragé, like are you tired?" he repeated with a dry smile.

"Ah, découragé! Well, peut-être un peu!"

No, I most definitely did not speak enough French. I had hoped that this job would improve my fluency; however, like all anglophones trying to pick up French from their coworkers, I instead used a manic language of hand and facial gestures to communicate various degrees of enthusiasm, diligence, perplexity, and apology, including but not limited to a high cock of the head with an open mouth (the What Was That?); a tense, determined squat holding a mop (the I'm On It), and a vigorous finger wag (the You Got Me There). Such miming usually succeeded in eliciting a thumbs-up, as it did now. "Make sure the plunger completely covers the hole," the chef said. As the motley-coloured liquid slunk away, I violently bobbed my head at him to demonstrate my gratitude.

I did not speak French, but I was trying to learn— fervently. Every word I plucked from conversation I whispered to myself over and over. When I stopped whispering a word too soon, it would dissipate like the grill's fumes in the stagnant air. It required focus for a word to take hold in my mind, but who could focus at thirty-five degrees? Our shirts had long since pasted to our chests, and one could dart into the walk-in freezer for reprieve only so many times. By now, the tap's hot water felt irritating, and the sole fan stood in the corner, looking back and forth as if it didn't get the joke. Wicking sweat from my eyelids, I stooped over the dishes like a goblin and, hoping that the chef wasn't listening, whispered to myself, "Découragé, découragé, découragé!"

I learned that day that this was becoming an unfortunate habit. I worked two shifts: from 9 a.m. to 3 p.m. and then from 6 p.m. to midnight. In between, I slipped into a nearby café-bookstore (thankfully air conditioned), stalking as lightly as possible through the entrance to minimize the squelch of my shoes. As I sat down at the far end of the countertop, I managed a surreptitious sniff of my armpit. There was no way to tell how bad the smell was, but it definitely wasn't good.

Avoiding eye contact with the cashier, who was smiling frantically, I sat down at the far end of the high countertop, as far as possible from the other customers, swigged several glasses of water, and opened *Les Fleurs du mal*. "Les monstres glapissants, hurlants, grognants, rampants / Dans la ménagerie infâme de nos vices." Definitely a lot of tricky *r* words, I thought, wiping the sheen from my upper lip and refilling my glass. *Hurlants, grognants, rampants ...* Only when I glanced up and saw the cashier and some customers looking quizzically at me did I become aware that my lips were moving. I sidled back out into the heat.

Getting home was a relief. I peeled off my sweat-heavy shirt and climbed into the cool shower. I looked at the dirt that clung tenaciously under my nails, giving them a little scrub and rinsing the grime from my forearms. How weird that my hands could be used for activities other than dishwashing. I continued to whisper the words I had learned throughout the day, but now a little more happily. At last, no one was listening, no one was watching.

My competence in French, it seemed, had in no way improved over the last month: I still mis-understood elementary vocabulary, still hacked out the guttural consonants, still prodded franco-phones to repeat jokes. But, all alone in the shower, I could pretend that French was my private lang-uage. After all, I couldn't really hope to stop babbling. The weather would be this hot all week.

Peak Performance
Eva Crocker

Squished on a floral sofa in Parc-Extension with a handful of strangers, I was instructed to begin making a noise you could really describe only as horny mewling. I went with something like the *mmm* you might make at the first bite of a delicious meal but angstier. This would escalate into wailing before easing into satisfied sighs.

It was my first rehearsal with the Fake Orgasm Choir. A queer performance artist named Coral Short was conducting us through four compositions they had written. They kneeled on the floor and waved their arms, getting us to build and then decrease the intensity of our moaning or the speed of our panting.

Before I arrived, I'd been told that no musical training was necessary. But I'd noticed a few worried glances when I admitted that, not only did I not know whether I was a soprano or an alto, I didn't even know what those words meant.

The rehearsal lasted two hours. Coral encouraged collaboration, getting excited when someone added improvised slurping noises. They recorded each song on their iPhone and we listened to it together, seriously discussing small changes to make in the next rendition. Before we left, Coral reminded us to wear all black on the night of the performance.

It was October, and I had just moved to Montreal from St. John's so my partner could attend grad school at Concordia. We arrived in late August with three suitcases and Bugs, our spunky Jack Russell terrier.

I was excited to live in what I'd heard was a weird and sexy city. People had told me that, since rent is cheaper in Montreal than in Toronto or Vancouver, it's easier to make art that might not be commercially viable. I knew of some of it: Dayna Danger's portraits of nude, oiled women holding antlers; a performance piece by Kama La Mackerel where the artist moved slowly, their body wrapped in wire and then a second layer of chicken wire.

After arriving, however, my routine involved working from home and wandering around Wesmount with the dog. I hadn't encountered much weirdness. Most afternoons, Bugs and I trudged along sterile streets lined with shops selling expensive leggings and brand-name parkas.

I was beginning to feel lonely. One day, on the way out of the house to meet school friends for lunch, my partner urged me to "get involved in something, maybe a book club at the library." That afternoon, I saw a Facebook post seeking participants for a Fake Orgasm Choir; it felt like a sign from the universe.

In elementary school, I was once asked to mouth the words in music class, and ever since, I've shied away from being involved in any kind of live performance. At the rehearsal, I did start to enjoy myself, coming up with dirty talk to volley into the barrage. I began with a timid "Don't stop" and worked my way up to "Yes, yes, wait, no, like before, a little more—yeah!"

But I didn't realize that, in just two weeks, the choir would be performing at an avant-garde event that prides itself on promoting "unclassifiable, unconventional, or experimental" artists. It was too late to turn back.

I met another choir member in the lobby of the ornate Rialto Theatre, both of us unsure where exactly to go. We began wandering around, listening for the choir.

The building was housing many of the festival's performances. We tiptoed through the back of a small theatre where an audience was rapt by a lit stage, empty except for a shower of small white feathers floating down from the ceiling. We followed a curling staircase up to a lobby where people were drinking from champagne flutes and then down to the basement, where someone was dancing in a set of butterfly wings made from what looked like unfurled hangers and a bedsheet.

Eventually, we heard the familiar sound of shrieking and followed the thundering climax to a dressing room where everyone applauded our late arrival. We'd made it just in time for the final run-through, and soon we trouped single file up a dark staircase.

We emerged onto a spotlit stage, about a hundred people staring up at us. For a moment, the thought of making sex noises at them felt nightmarish. Then we formed a loose semicircle and Coral stood, arms raised high. Everyone moaned in unison. As the next song's panting opening crescendoed into howling, I caught the eye of the woman next to me. We exchanged a gleeful look.

I realized I'd stepped through a portal, right into freaky Montreal. I was so glad I came.

Reading the Signs
Deborah Ostrovsky

He said he'd leave if the Parti Québécois's Charter of Values passed. It was the fall of 2013, and we were sitting in my living room, watching the intense political debates happening around then about the charter. Both of us had just entered unanticipated new life stages. My friend had received a cancer diagnosis. I had a baby rolling around on the rug, pulling the cat's tail, oblivious to the pundits on TV discussing a law designed to determine who would be allowed to teach her and the religious symbols those teachers could wear.

He would find it painful to leave, he said—to face a diagnosis in some other city. It would be less painful, though, than staying in Montreal, a place he adored even as it became increasingly divided. Illness or no illness, he couldn't tolerate the spirit of what was happening. As a man of colour who had confronted discrimination. As a man who had lived and worked just about everywhere but had finally chosen Quebec as his home. Then the cancer went into remission. So did talk of the law.

But, before long, the cancer spread to his liver. Then, a few years later, clusters of mutated cells metastasized everywhere. Inoperable tumours usurped the strength that his body should have regained after chemo, radiation, and finally immunotherapy. God knows what other treatments he refrained from telling us about. To protect friends, or himself, from our fears.

Another election and more talk of religious symbols. But, this time, with my friend's health suddenly taking another downturn, it was too late for him to think about moving. I rented a new office near his apartment on Rue Parthenais, secretly hoping it would give me a legitimate excuse to check in every day. I loved him deeply, platonically, and I would have done anything to help. I carved out elaborate fantasies about prolonging his future: he would get well enough to meet a woman who deserved him. They would have a child of their own. We would all walk together through Parc La Fontaine with our strollers. Go to the wading pool. The bouncy castles in the Old Port. Anywhere at all.

In reality, he was secretive, telling me nothing about his love life or plummeting sperm count. I spied online to glean these details. He joined a group for men with infertility, a side effect of his cancer treatment. A hospital newsletter quoted him saying he was terrified of putting a lover through the ups and downs of disease.

By the time the Coalition Avenir Québec introduced the new religious-neutrality bill, in the spring, I was sure there would have been more obvious signs, portents, augurs to prepare me for my friend's demise. I invited him to a party; he declined. Treatment that day. "I'll be sleeping like a baby!" he emailed. Five days later, he was dead.

I sat in my office until midnight, refreshing the web page of his online obituary over and over, praying this was all a cruel joke. I stood in my office stairwell, at a window overlooking Parthenais where it meets Rue Masson, an industrial-looking corner with a trade school and train tracks that seem to lead nowhere. I made myself believe that I saw him, resurrected, shuffling from pain but coming to visit me, crossing where Masson suddenly turns into multiple lanes.

I searched for signs of my friend everywhere in the city. I visited a shiatsu therapist in a dilapidated building on Avenue des Pins. She pressed her hand on my stomach as I sobbed. She encouraged me to read Carl Jung and to try talking to the dead. Many nights, I lay in bed next to my husband, silently pleading with our friend to answer us. Was he safe on the other side? I kept having the same agonizing dream: him standing on my stoop, ringing my doorbell. I couldn't answer. I was paralyzed.

Two months after the secularism law passed under the new government, there was finally a memorial at a private club. It was near the airport, with bucolic gardens. How fitting that, as planes flew overhead, we gathered in a Victorian sitting room, eating canapés, watching a widescreen TV, a photo montage: our friend getting his pilot's licence; him cycling; him— an ex–Seventh Day Adventist—handsome and wearing a yarmulke, smiling in a synagogue with friends I didn't know.

"Had he converted?" asked someone from out of town, surprised.

"No. Yes. Maybe. Who knows?" I said as the slideshow rolled on, the airplanes soaring above us, a city emptied of signs down below.

Melting Away
Jeff Miller

First you lay the strips of Spencer steak on the grill. On top, circles of pepperoni. Next comes shredded mozzarella, which melts and holds the whole mess together. Slide the long metal spatula underneath and place it on a toasted sub bun. With onions and hot peppers, the Sousmarin Jimmy Style was named for the previous owner of the place that became Dépanneur Le Pick Up.

The grill predated everything. Before the tropical sunset wallpaper. Before the jam-preserving workshops and the zine rack. Before craft beer and art installations. Before the tech takeover of Mile End pushed the freaks farther north. Way before the words "Mile-Ex" had ever been spoken. When Montreal art punks Bernie and Penny bought the little wood-panelled casse-croûte-slash-dépanneur, in the summer of 2008, and I became their first employee, there was the grill and the Jimmy Style sub. Jimmy still lived upstairs and came down for coffee and smokes every day.

The burgers and subs of the original menu

sizzled while clumps of fashionable pulled pork hissed and trendy halloumi tanned. Jimmy hadn't run the grill much during the previous few years, and now that it was back on, the locals were returning. A big part of the business was running deliveries to meat packers and auto-detailing shops. Alongside them were artists, queers, punks, and assorted weirdos—our friends. Things melted together: cheese, meat, bun; past, present, future.

This neighbourhood between Little Italy, Mile End, and Parc-Ex always had an ill-defined quality: a tangle of mixed-used zoning, homes interspersed with garages, warehouses, and textiles factories. But it was far from a time capsule. By the early 2000s, posh architect-designed duplexes, art galleries, and the offices of fashion brands and book publishers had arrived along with the aggressive condoization and gentrification felt across Montreal.

Le Pick Up emerged from Jimmy's dep just as, in the 1980s, Jimmy's Greek immigrant father had transformed it from the original casse-croûte, Chez Maurice. Chez Maurice had been started in the 1960s, on the corner of Alexandra and Waverly, to serve local factory workers. The ways the neighbourhood would continue to change were only dimly apparent to us at the time.

Four days a week that first summer, I closed alone. When the Player's cigarettes clock above the door read 6:15 p.m., I turned the grill's heat dial to max, letting the day's gunk sizzle.

Around the same time, Dougie would come in through the open door. His silver hair was pomaded, his face lined. He lived across the street and was in a few times every day, looking for matches or two litres of cola or something to do. He would sit at the counter and tell me jokes as I poured his after-supper mug of drip coffee.

Jean would arrive next, his beat-up truck carrying an electric radiator or a pile of old pipes. The two would leave an empty stool between them, dissecting the Habs' prospects for the coming season in joual. They didn't seem to mind the waft of greasy steam as I began my assault on the grill with soapy water.

Every few minutes, someone would come through the door. A young woman in a neon band T-shirt playing a show that night at Il Motore up the street, looking for a snack. A black-clad bike messenger grabbing a beer from the glass-door fridge. The quiet woman from the single-resident-occupancy building down the block who paid for a can of tuna with a handful of change. Or the elderly Italian regular in a blazer and trilby who yelled "uovo!" as he walked toward the eggs. Our Haitian neighbour from two doors down bought cigarettes and food for his cat, who waited for him in her tuxedo on the dep's front step before following him home.

In between, I scraped and cursed. Finally, I turned the grill dial all the way down to zero. The grill and the people are what I remember most about my two years there. I loved being part of the neighbourhood—ringing up people's essentials, trading our feelings on the weather.

The foodie media and *New York Times* attention eventually brought a different lunch crowd, and Le Pick Up was a vector for a "new" neighbourhood some started calling Mile-Ex. As tech now tries to swallow the area whole, the undefinable neighbourhood I knew is threatened, and it's hard to imagine what it will be like in another twelve years.

But, for now, the flat-top grill remains—not as a memorial but as a point of continuity in a city recklessly selling itself to the highest bidder.

Highs and Lows
André Picard

When I glance out the window of my home office, I see the iconic cross atop Mount Royal. The base of "the mountain"—as Montrealers call the modest triple-peaked hill in the middle of the island—is 771 metres from my front door. (The kind of trivial information you know when you're a runner-slash-data-geek with a GPS-equipped watch.)

Mount Royal has been my unofficial backyard (or, more precisely, front yard) for the past three decades. I run there in the morning. I walk across it on my way to work and home again. When out-of-towners visit, the first order of business is a jaunt to the Kondiaronk Belvedere, where there is a breathtaking view of downtown Montreal, complete with its Leonard Cohen mural, and the Saint Lawrence River—a ritual that makes you feel you've earned the subsequent visit to Schwartz's or La Banquise.

I've always taken the mountain for granted. But COVID-19 has given me a new appreciation of this oasis.

As a health journalist living in the epicentre of the Canadian outbreak, my life has been consumed by COVID-19. I've spent every day since mid-January glued to the computer, watching and writing the news, perhaps with a little more sense than the regular reader of how bad it could get.

Thankfully, I have an antidote to the stress. By the time I stroll past two Portuguese chicken restaurants (Romados and Portugalia) and I can see the trees of Mount Royal, the anxiety has already lifted.

I could navigate Chemin Olmsted, the 5.5-kilometre-long winding dirt road that leads from the Sir George-Étienne Cartier monument to the cross, with my eyes closed—though not necessarily without the occasional stumble, and I have the scars to prove it. I know where to go to watch the Cooper's hawks soar and hunt pigeons, the spots where the chickadees will feed from your hand, the area where you might spot a shy red fox, the muddy bogs where kids can catch salamanders, and the meandering forest paths that make you feel far from the city.

For early morning runners like myself, the pandemic has changed our routine very little. The coronavirus-related backlash is laughable; runners are social distancers by nature, loners who exchange polite nods in passing, not germ bombs.

What is most noticeable during my morning jaunts is what is no longer there. The playgrounds are closed to children. No one is staking out a picnic table for a birthday or family gathering. Access to paths and stairs—even the lung-bursting 339-step staircase up the escarpment—is blocked with unsightly police tape, though this tape is routinely torn down. Montrealers are not, by nature, rule followers; in a city where stop signs are largely decorative, it takes more than a bit of tape to keep people from their beloved Mount Royal.

The giant eyesore of a parking lot near Smith House is mercifully empty. Tour buses are no longer idling and disgorging hordes. That seems to have left the raccoons and squirrels perplexed and scrawny; they have always counted on the tourists, not the locals, to feed them.

Santa Cruz Church and community centre, a nearby hub for the Portuguese community, is eerily quiet. The field where football and soccer teams battle for supremacy is locked tight.

Tam-Tams, a popular Sunday gathering for drummers and dancers, has fallen prey to rules of physical distancing. The overwhelming smell of pot is no longer there, though a few die-hards have tried to keep the toking-and-drumming tradition alive—at a two-metre distance, of course.

Yet you can't totally escape the grim reminders that death and suffering are close by. Four hospitals are built on the flanks of Mount Royal, and as many cemeteries. The mountain has been a burial ground for centuries, if not millennia, and is home to Canada's largest cemetery, Notre-Dame-des-Neiges. Given the COVID-19 carnage, the cemeteries are busy yet closed to visitors. One morning, I watched a family, flowers in hand, stare mournfully through the fence.

As the lockdown drags on, many more stir-crazy people begin to flock to Mount Royal. The warmer spring days arrive along with police and crowd control. There is not enough room to contain the angst, even in a 200-hectare park.

When I head up there on a weekend with family, there is palpable concern, if not fear, in the air. Masks are commonplace. Walkers try to give a wide berth to other walkers, and angry words are exchanged—often in an impressive multitude of languages—when someone comes too close.

Still, I know that, the next morning, around sunrise, it will be quiet again. That 771-metre path to freedom will beckon, and beyond it, momentary mountain bliss.

Out of the Cave
Galadriel Watson

In the mid-1980s, my friend Alison and I spent our days sitting in space and sunlight, in classrooms with big windows overlooking mature trees and well-kept lawns. Our all-girls high school was in Westmount: Miss Edgar's and Miss Cramp's School. Later in the day, though, we'd ditch it for masses of bodies, second-hand oxygen, and artificial lights, all enclosed in concrete. Our target: downtown Montreal's Place Bonaventure, a bunker-like complex that combined an exhibition hall, a trade centre, offices, a transportation hub, and a shopping mall.

I lived a few blocks from school, but Alison lived on the South Shore. Rather than going home after class, I'd accompany her by bus and metro to Place Bonaventure so she could catch her final transfer. On the jolting train, we'd wrap her one long scarf around both our necks, a physical manifestation of how inseparable we were. We'd laugh obnoxiously loudly at our inside jokes, undoubtedly annoying other passengers.

Then, from the bowels of the metro, we'd stumble into the bowels of Place Bonaventure—one of Montreal's many subterranean spots that let you shop, eat, and travel without ever rising for air. Waiting for Alison's bus, we loitered in the mall. We rummaged through racks of records; a youthful Madonna smouldered from the covers. I bought waist-length strings of plastic pearls, very trendy. Later—in CEGEP and with a part-time job in this same complex—I purchased tiny diamond earrings for my boyfriend's birthday. After I gave them to him, I selfishly convinced him that he should give me one back.

It was that job that popped into my mind when I read, in early June 2020, that Place Bonaventure's exhibition hall was closing. Immediately, I felt myself clacking up concrete steps in navy inch-high heels and a navy polyester skirt suit. I was heading to a trade fair to register the day's exhibitors—something to do with crafts. Maybe books. The hall's ribbed concrete columns rose far overhead to the concrete-beamed ceiling, pendant lights blazing. It had been made vibrant with booths and brochures, with echoing voices and rambling footsteps. I remember being stymied by some of the French as I welcomed people and pointed the way.

Overall, though, I managed okay.

This stint was one of my many teenage jobs: secretary for an interior designer, clothing-store salesperson, waitress. Place Bonaventure's locker-lined staff room seemed to be in the deepest, darkest depths of the building. It felt like the interminable hallway burrowed into a cave.

Today, the only cave-like settings near me are actual, stalagmite-filled caves. Long gone, too, are the job, boyfriend, and friend. I haven't been to Place Bonaventure for at least three decades. Born in Alberta, I spent about ten years in Montreal before returning west, where I ultimately settled in small-town British Columbia.

In 2017, I vacationed for a few days in Montreal and remembered what I'd been missing. A tour of several metro stations reminded me how much the city loves its concrete.

I now know the name of Place Bonaventure's imposing architectural style. Brutalism, stark and blocky. Poured concrete on the floors, up the walls, in the rafters. Chilly, sombre caverns made by human hands. When construction finished, in 1967, its 3.1 million square feet of floor space—above ground and below—made it the world's largest concrete building.

Those days I spent milling and working in Place Bonaventure feel very far away right now. In time. In location. In other ways. No one's gathering for trade fairs this year. Will massive, elbow-knocking events ever happen again?

According to *La Presse*, Place Bonaventure's exhibition hall was already planning on closing its doors in 2020, but the pandemic sped it up—it had to cancel a couple of springtime gatherings. The building's website says it has hosted over 3,000 events since it opened, with many millions of visitors.

Even the Madonna-adorned mall is pretty much gone: it shrank drastically in a 1998 reno to make room for more offices. When I read about it, I was shocked to discover that construction workers had replaced swaths of concrete with windows. They fractured the cave to let in light.

To me, though, Place Bonaventure will always remain deeply underground. It was a place for dawdling before heading home, alone, to face homework. It was cheap clothes. It was teenage giddiness. It may have been dark and brutal, but we liked it anyway.

Vanishing Act
Valerie Silva

After spending months mostly inside, the border between the skin of my thighs and the fabric of my couch had become indistinct. One Saturday afternoon in May 2020, I finally took this as my cue to venture outside. It wasn't an original idea: the warm weather had drawn Montrealers out of their pandemic cocoons in droves. Once outdoors, in the sun, I was tempted to stay there, but it wasn't the euphoria I had expected. I was wary of the proximity of strangers. Locked into a cycle of anxious thoughts and craving a return to privacy, I ducked into an alley to make my escape.

To my surprise, I instead found myself face to face with twenty or so people in wild costumes. They skipped, laughed, and shouted down the alley to the tune of "Twist and Shout," which blared from the speakers accompanying their socially distanced fleet. A clown in Victorian face paint and a feathered velvet blazer shuffled behind them on stilts. A family of bikers, their helmets decorated with flowers, followed in line. Taking a step back,

I watched as two men operated a cardboard owl marionette who looked about as stupefied as I was. I swivelled around at the sound of cheers, realizing that an audience had grown behind me at the alley's entrance.

Montrealers have always made the most of our communal ruelles, but this was next level. Spectators whooped and applauded from third-storey balconies. A father scooped up his small son to watch from a window. As the procession trickled into the alley across the road, a man in a train conductor's getup, propped on a unicycle and juggling knives, blew me a kiss goodbye.

Montreal's reputation as an epicentre of the nouveau cirque was solidified in the 1980s with the formation of its best-known export, Cirque du Soleil. The movement was predicated on humans, not animals, and storylines, not stunts. Its success spun out of a maelstrom of forces, including Montreal's history of street performance and a Quebec government vying for national independence. During that decade, the province began channelling funds to projects that would prove its distinctiveness as a culture. Cirque made out big.

If Montreal is a circus town, then Hochelaga-Maisonneuve is its green room. The neighbourhood's relatively low rents make it a haven for aspiring performers of the nouveau cirque. Amateur slackliners and unicyclists are scattered among the area's pawn shops, vacant storefronts, and turn-of-the-century triplexes. The borough is also home to La Caserne, a fire-station-turned-recreation-centre where acrobats under thirty find their feet before joining well-known troupes around town.

Like every other institution that relies on touch, La Caserne went on a pandemic-prompted hiatus in spring 2020. Cirque du Soleil, meanwhile, laid off nearly 5,000 people, about 95 percent of its workforce, and sought a massive cash injection. Montreal's circus performers, rarely all in town at once, were expediently shipped back home from tours around the world.

As for the procession I had witnessed, it was the culmination of industry friends suddenly finding themselves out of work and living within a couple of blocks of one another. They formed Bonheur Mobile, French for "mobile happiness," to punctuate weeks of listless confinement and bring some levity to their community—one that had long fostered their talents but perhaps hadn't actually had the opportunity to enjoy them. (A ticket to Cirque, after all, can cost hundreds of dollars.)

Eventually, the troupe got roped into performing all over the city—while staying always unannounced, always in motion. Still, the back channels around Joliette station, narrow corridors of cracking asphalt and untended grass that give way to back porches and kitchen windows, are where Bonheur Mobile got its start.

Over the next few months, I saw videos of the procession in matching costumes, performing well-rehearsed and cohesive routines. These performances lacked the scrappy thematic mishmash that had given those early gatherings the impression of a family pooling their resources for a basement talent show. It might not have made sense, but at the time, it felt right. Passing through the alleys today, you would never know that they had once been filled with furloughed circus performers trying to ratchet up morale. The crowd has dispersed, the troupe has packed its things, not even one errant turquoise feather has been left behind as proof. Yet the possibility that something unexpected might transpire has kept me alert as I walk, kept me away from the cognitive acrobatics in my head.

Queer Atmosphere
Eli Tareq El Bechelany-Lynch

"ETA ten minutes," my friend Hunter texts me. I know that means they'll probably be here in twenty, but I don't mind. I've always felt comfortable sitting alone at Notre Dame des Quilles.

On any given night at the queer bar, I might see three people I sort of know, someone I briefly dated, and my best friend's horrible ex—all while some straight person drunkenly tries to bowl in the wooden lanes the place is named after. Tonight, it's especially busy, so I sling my jacket over one of the tables at the back to guard my spot.

After Hunter arrives, we try to decide if the queers at the table across from us are on a first date. Just when we agree that it seems a bit awkward, one of them sits on the other's lap and they start making out. We look away to give them some privacy. I can't help but notice the person at the ATM directly beside the couple doing their best not to stare, face almost comically focused on remembering their PIN.

When I was eighteen, my new friends from Concordia dragged me up to the no-frills queer bar in Little Italy for the first time. Living downtown, we'd never made it past Saint-Laurent metro, let alone onto the orange line. My friends were all queer; I wasn't sure about my sexuality. For months, I had been trying to decide whether wanting to make out with girls made me, maybe, not straight.

I didn't realize that night how often I'd find myself in the glow of NDQ's mood lighting in the years to come. Singing a duet of "Islands in the Stream" with my friend Griffin on a country-themed karaoke Sunday, using the bowling lanes as a makeshift stage. Spilling a drink on myself as I nervously tried to impress my current partner, Felix, while they made me laugh. Sitting alone, attempting to read Larissa Lai's *The Tiger Flu* despite the noise while my friend Yousra participated in lesbian speed dating.

For those of us who haven't been interested in braving the cis- and male-centric energy of the Village, NDQ has been the place to go. While Montreal may be known for its large queer community, the city hasn't been kind to our queer spaces. Bar after bar has shut down in recent years, from Cabaret Playhouse to Royal Phoenix. But the hole-in-the-wall in Little Italy has remained reliably packed: you can count on finding friends sharing pizzas hot out of the oven in the back, dates sitting on the floor for cult movie screenings, and strangers hooking up on the dance floor.

That all changed when the pandemic hit, of course. When we think of what this time has stolen from so many people, being able to meet casually at your favourite queer bar might feel low on the priority list. But, if this year has taught me anything, it's how to mourn things big and small without guilt, honouring even the minor losses that affect our daily lives.

The queer bar has always been a place for chosen family to gather. That's something I miss, especially as governments continue to set pandemic restrictions with traditional family structures in mind. This limited understanding of what a family can look like has complicated the ways queers in the city have been able to see and support one another. It's ironic given that we've been navigating conversations around consent, safety, and relationship dynamics for years.

Even so, we've been finding new ways to stay connected. Now, instead of meeting at NDQ, my friends and I walk side by side in Parc Jarry, two metres apart, wading through snow and ice. Sometimes we watch the colourful sunsets that start at 4 p.m., the most dazzling ones visible from Parc-Ex. Just a short walk away, the bar is there, waiting for our safe return.

These days, I've been dreaming of going back to NDQ and getting to hear Lenore, Montreal's queer celebrity karaoke host, call my name up onstage. I'd sing a song I've been practising in Felix's living room, like Tracy Chapman's "Talkin' 'bout a Revolution" or the Goo Goo Dolls' "Iris." I can almost hear the crowd of queers cheering me on.

Good Neighbours
Nour Abi-Nakhoul

As my partner, Ziya, and I stroll down Saint-Zotique, our route turns wavy with the gentle detours we make around other pedestrians. We give slower walkers wide berths of careful distance, hopping down curbs or around trees to avoid the close proximity of others.

In the winter, it was difficult to even see the people I was trying to keep away from thanks to the fog that my mask sent up into my glasses. But, as the warm weather has gifted clarity to once slush-clogged streets, it has also gifted clarity to my line of sight. This is important because I like to scan the street for my friends, the only neighbours I can be close with right now—the cats of Montreal.

I settled into Montreal in the dead cold of winter at the end of 2019, after ferrying my books, clothes, and cats in a cube truck over Highway 401 from Toronto. All my prospects in Toronto were drying up. At some point, you get frustrated with moving every six months, each room smaller than the last.

I'd visited Montreal dozens of times, most recently to see my long-distance sweetheart. Ziya regaled me with stories of their Montreal adventures—exhilarating evenings running into friends at arts events, relaxing afternoons in parks and on patios. I was seduced by the idea of a city with a culture grounded in a sort of laid-back eccentricity. Wooed over by the promises of a fun and community-oriented city, I decided to make the move. I wanted a place where people walked languorously and waved to you from balconies. Where people had balconies to begin with.

I waited out the winter like a patient animal in hibernation. Every couple of weeks, someone new would ask me how I was adjusting to the city, and I'd explain that I hadn't managed to experience much of it yet. *Wait until the summer*, they'd invariably respond. *Montreal in the summer is truly something ...* And they'd trail off, gazing into the distance with a half smile like a drowsy person recalling some faraway, delectably sweet dream.

I waited and waited, fiddling my fingers. Then the winter thawed, and out of its darkness jumped the terrible fiend of COVID-19, stealing away any promises of a genuine Montreal summer. Montreal has become as emotionally stunted as a bad exboyfriend because of the pandemic. The primary feeling it relays is anxiety. For a city that prides itself on its eccentricity and depth of character, this suppression is rather miserable.

But I've managed to excavate the true personality of my new home through my tiny mewling neighbours: the city's cats, whom I've gotten to know extremely well. There's the beautiful tortoiseshell Croquette, who lies outside the hair salon all summer; Beanut, the skinny tabby who screams and runs over to say hi when she sees you; and the one I affectionately call Big Guy, who is indeed a massively big guy. (Aside from Croquette, whose name we gleaned from her collar, we nickname them all in the spur of the moment.)

Montreal's cats are as ubiquitous and as prone to suddenly appearing in strange places as the city's ever-present construction cones. They don't just provide solace through the social isolation and terror of this anxiety-inflected year; they're also a microcosm of the character of the city—lazily friendly, personable, disinclined to meaningless labour, and not a little bit odd. Gently presenting my hand for every cat I see to sniff, I feel hope for the resilience of Montreal's personality.

"Let's go see if Beanut's out today," Ziya says, motioning toward the street where our favourite cat lives. We spot our beautiful little friend napping regally on the winding stairs of a duplex. "Beanut!" we both yell, and the tabby perks up and gallops over to us, pressing her head into our hands affectionately.

We coo and babble at her before saying our goodbyes and continuing down the street, feeling as though we just had a happy spontaneous run-in with a neighbour. For a moment, it's like the personality and sociability of the neighbourhood is still present, just shrunk down to a tiny four-legged size.

Past Curfew
Alex Manley

The way people make mistakes—unconscious missteps of the tongue, Freudian slips and mis-attributions—is a fascinating trap door into the way they really feel. So it was revealing to me this summer when, conjuring up a memory from May 28, 2021—the night Montreal's months-long curfew was finally lifted—I referred to it as New Year's Eve.

Of course, there were similarities: the fireworks spider-webbing the sky, the drinks with friends, the atmosphere, which, if not quite "anything goes," was at least "a few more things go." And, of course, the big communal countdown.

There was also the fact that, for a week or so afterward, it was common to swap stories with friends about what you'd done that fateful night: who you'd been with and how late, finally, you'd crawled into bed. The fact that the countdown—What to call such an occasion? Curfew Year's Eve? Le Couv-el An?—occurred at 9:30 p.m. in late May and not at the tail end of December was little more than an asterisk.

In the days leading up to the curfew lifting, my partner, Blair, and I had juggled our desires (stay out late, see friends) and boundaries (avoid crowds, keep outdoors) before settling on a plan that felt right: we'd climb Mount Royal with our friends Molly and Dane. When Molly met us at the base of the monument, around 9 p.m., her joke about wanting to perform open-air burlesque felt apt. We were shedding layers of something—inhibition, fear, the hoary closed-offness that had defined the winter for so many Montrealers, the enforced emptiness of our nights, the numbing sameness of our days.

The clearest sign that something was in the air was an unexpected addition to our party. A woman about our age sat down near Molly and started chatting with her, and before long, Hallie was a bona fide member of our climbing expedition. When Dane arrived, he greeted her no differently than he might have an old friend, and as Hallie joined in our reminiscences about bygone cheaper rents, I realized I'd forgotten that you could still talk to strangers, still find common ground through happenstance.

Before we'd gone far, we came upon a scene that felt stripped from a dream—a golden glow, a thumping beat, a few dozen ravers going wild, packed tight in a way that felt distinctly unsafe, a glowing ember of carefree revelry in the mountain's enveloping dark. We were drawn to it despite ourselves. We hadn't seen dancing in so long. I breathed a sigh of relief when we returned to the path and kept moving, unnerved by the secret forest ball's magnetic pull.

When we reached the stairs toward the Kondiaronk Belvedere, I tore up the steps, taking them two at a time. It was a thoughtless move, and a few minutes passed before Blair joined me. Hallie, she said, hadn't been able to manage the stairs—earlier, she'd mentioned a disability, but she had gamely tried to stick with her newfound friends. After a brief discussion, Dane had offered to walk her back down to the street.

Eventually, Molly came into view, and she, Blair, and I made our way to the belvedere. Indoors every night, I'd missed the fullness of the pitch-black sky. It felt like an old friend. Around us, the average person on the belvedere seemed to be about twenty and in full party mode. Portable speakers blared tinny songs that shifted between familiar and not. But we'd made it. The city lay glittering below us.

Dane returned a half hour later or so, and the four of us caught up before the night's unofficial grand finale: a half-dozen men riding motorized single-wheel contraptions, zipping around the belvedere's circumference, wearing matching outfits criss-crossed with glowing LED lights. The crowd roared its approval. This city really does love a unicycle.

Soon afterward, we made our way back to the infamous wooden steps. I checked the time. It was 11:56 p.m. Behind us, the youth partied on.

In retrospect, perhaps I was right to remember that night as New Year's Eve, if only because the countdown chorus that rang out through the air had been leading us to a transitional moment, a point after which things would be different in a way much more tangible than the typical shift from one calendar year to the next.

After that night, we felt free again. We got our second doses. Park hangs and back-patio dinners followed, and eventually even travel plans began to flow, like the ice melting at the end of a long winter.

The Plaza
Ziya Jones

My first memories of Montreal's Plaza St-Hubert are as weird, liminal, and hazy as the commercial strip itself. I first trekked to the plaz (as I like to call it) in 2015 to attend a queer dance party. I recall strolling drunkenly along the four-block strip, past anime stores, wig shops, and retailers advertising $50 prom dresses. My destination was Bar Le Félix, a short-lived club that tried to capture the cachet of Berlin nightlife by having two shirtless bouncers in animal masks confiscate everyone's phones at the door.

Past that point, the night comes to me in fragments: a room inside the venue that was completely empty save for a blow-up mattress on the floor; a single-stall bathroom with a large window right next to the toilet; my friend making out with a man inexplicably dressed in a full cowboy outfit.

I do remember this, though: I fucking loved it. I started to return to the plaz regularly, in the light of day, to wrap myself in its chaos. I found it calming to amble along, trying to identify that week's most tempting deal (a tank top emblazoned with *I flex for sex*, only $2!) or most intense window display (two mannequins dressed for a Renaissance fair next to a giant white horse). The controlled mayhem was a welcome distraction from the stressful unpredictability of regular life.

The plaz wasn't always so bric-à-brac. Saint-Hubert began to turn commercial in the 1920s and grew popular over the next three decades. In 1951, the iconic chicken chain of the same name opened its very first location on the strip. A few years later, merchants formed an official association, which helped steer the plaz into its most prosperous decade. By the sixties, Saint-Hubert was the second most important commercial strip in all of Quebec, next to Sainte-Catherine.

Its reign was short-lived. The street was already falling out of favour with shoppers when a bulky green awning was added over the sidewalks, in the eighties. The structure was considered an eyesore by both residents and visitors. The plaz remained a commercial area, but as the new millennium dawned, bargain shops settled in and transitioned it into a junk-lover's paradise—like gentrification in reverse.

By the time I arrived in the city, Saint-Hubert was changing once again. Storefronts shuttered steadily at first, then rapidly. Between 2018 and 2020, eighty of the plaza's 400 businesses closed. Eighty-nine new ones sprouted up in their place during the same period, their flavour largely changed. Cheap taco joints and stores selling knock-off Nike made way for pastel-coloured dessert spots and natural wine bars.

The transformation of the plaza was helped along by the pandemic, which took a toll on small businesses citywide, as well as by the city's $50 million revitalization project, which left the strip under construction for nearly three years. Anti-gentrification activists began to sound the alarm over BIPOC business owners being priced out of the strip.

Still, the march of gentrification is rarely clean and linear. During the pandemic, Black-owned bookstore Librairie Racines opened a plaza location. Decades-old businesses like Radio St-Hubert and Le Roi du Smoked Meat have stayed put. And the area remains a hub for the city's Latinx community. Cruising spot Sauna St-Hubert—one of the only bathhouses in the city that welcomed trans women—shuttered a few years back, but the street is still home to multiple fetish stores, a porn theatre, and a swingers' club.

The plaz also maintains some of its chaotic spirit. When its latest renovation was officially unveiled last summer, a group of city engineers on strike disrupted mayor Valérie Plante's speech, protesting loudly for most of the launch event. Soon afterward, a plaza barbershop made the news after its window was shattered by a couple making out passionately up against it.

Walking Saint-Hubert now, I take stock of its post-lockdown state. I see at least three new places to buy overpriced candles, sure. But there's also the shoe store with the owner who told me he lends out his stock for free to anyone who needs them for photo shoots. There's 100,000 Jeans, a boutique that somehow sells basically zero denim. There's a store that's just called Style. There's a store that's just called Swag City.

There's my hope that, no matter what the plaz becomes next, it stays at least a little bit weird.

The Shape of a Scene
Rosie Long Decter

Walking along the green path, I'm filled with a predictable anxiety. The show has already started, and I'm going to miss the opening act. They're earnest and jangly, good for a sun going down. I think, *Who starts a show at six?* But I know that, in a pandemic, the rules of nightlife come unhooked from time and space.

I check my texts for more information. Who's there? Have they gone on yet? And where, actually, am I going? I feel nineteen, like I'm showing up at a DIY venue to admire the outfits and scroll on my phone. The path curves west along the train tracks and I look up at the Rosemont overpass. A fuzzy tone drifts through the air.

I played my first local show in 2014, the year after I moved to Montreal. The more I went to gigs here, the more I got to know the contours of a scene: which venues had reliable sound, who would put you on guest list, who would never remember your name. The thrill of a set that catches you off guard.

I was grateful to live in a city with reasonable rent and warehouse space, where there was always something going on, even in twenty below.

"A scene resists deciphering," writes cultural scholar Will Straw, "in part, because it mobilizes local energies and moves these energies in multiple directions." For Straw, scenes indicate an excess— some surplus energy that cannot be channelled into the standard spaces of school, work, home. Moving through this excess, I often felt like I didn't have the right look or taste to be showing up at all. I blamed the discomfort on Montreal, a city too busy being cool, and admired people who seemed to go from show to show with ease, like they had it all mapped out.

Local musician Joni Sadler, a friend who passed away suddenly in 2021, built on Straw's work in her master's thesis, a study of experimental artists. Her interviews with musicians found that they often valued social and cultural capital more than economic definitions of success. "A healthy music scene can lead to a shared sense of purpose," Joni wrote. "What this may risk, in some cases, is the conscious or unconscious formation of boundaries at the perimeters of a music scene." Scenes can be both liberating and lonely.

As I got older, my experiences in music started

adding up to something more than a series of nights gone well or poorly. In 2017, Joni hired me to work at CKUT, McGill's campus radio station. I spent my days listening to piles of mail-in CDs with her and the volunteers, getting to know Montreal's expansive jazz, francophone, and hip-hop scenes. Outside of the station, I played in more projects while my friends worked for local festivals and promoters. It felt like something close to community.

Communities, of course, are never static. As rent in Montreal rises and the city focuses on large-scale ventures, the shape of a scene changes. I can name at least eight independent venues that have recently shut down or been bought out. Sometimes scenes are broken by their own internal logics too. Prioritizing cultural and social capital over economics opens up space for alternative modes of art and care. It can also foster competition and betrayal. Informal hierarchies emerge; abuse goes unchecked; patterns of marginalization persist. And scenes change when people change. Some of my friends have left town, some have stopped playing music, and some have stopped talking to me, or vice versa.

Through it all, people keep making shit. They book shows and rent generators and convince opening acts to go on at 6 p.m. so that the headliners might play before the cops show up. And so that I will leave my house on a Friday night.

Scenes are shaped by material circumstances, but their essential excess comes from people. Like my friend Joni, who believed very much in strange sounds and always opened the perimeters to let someone new in the shape. There's no one version of a community. Excesses spill across boundaries.

I keep walking west down the tracks, following the distortion. A group emerges near a makeshift stage, and the sound is huge and enthralling. I find a spot by a tree, open a beer, and look around at the crowd until a familiar face appears.

All in the Family
Anna Leventhal

The first time I met John, he was wearing a poncho, dropping off some mail at the apartment I was house-sitting. When I opened the door, we both went "Oh!" because we were both expecting someone else. A year later, it was my apartment and he was my super. Then he wasn't the super anymore—I found that out because I called him about my water pressure and he screamed that it wasn't his problem. "DO YOU KNOW WHAT DYING IS, ANNA?" He later apologized and lived another five years.

Our building had three floors and a basement, fourteen units all told. John was in number five, with a balcony that opened onto the back courtyard, where I locked my bike. It was rare to come home and not find him there, smoking and chatting with whoever walked by.

The other units were occupied by a rotating cast. Some of my best friends lived there, and we became close in a way you only can with people with whom you share a poorly soundproofed Montreal apartment building. We were bonded by the kind of intimacy that comes from hearing someone's music and toilet flushes and sex noises and knowing they can hear yours, from being in someone's space when you can't help it, not just for fun and companionship but when they're sick or hurting or their cat's been run over in the night. We expect to find this intimacy in families, but it grows in other places too.

John was Scottish by origin and still had his accent. He was an actor. He told us he had once performed in a production of *Waiting for Godot* directed by Beckett himself. After coming to Canada, he'd gone into movies and TV and had played everything from a spy to an elder of Sparta to a corpse. He was the kind of actor who could find work well into his seventies. He had that kind of face. Iconoclastic, versatile.

After a stroke, he started depending on his neighbours more. We'd roll cigarettes for him, pick up groceries, bring him "the usual," a ham sandwich and a latte, from the Italian café-bar on the corner, where they knew his order. In fall of 2015, he went into the hospital. He'd been in and out a few times over the past few years. He was convinced that the doctors had done something to him, left a piece of medical equipment in his body. He told us not to visit.

It was mid-September when I got a call from Derek, who lived in the apartment across the hall from John. He told me John had died. I didn't feel surprised, only a sort of long-off sorrow, like looking at a lighthouse from far away.

We held a memorial in the backyard, stringing Derek's Christmas lights across the cable lines. Our neighbour Justin cut every flower from his garden and brought them over by the armload. We put a picture of John on the chair where he'd sat and chain-smoked and sung songs to his dog, strewed it with flowers, and lit a candle. People from all over the neighbourhood came. Pamela and Brendan each performed a song in his honour. Justin retold some of John's favourite jokes, and Kandis read a letter she'd written him. When it was my turn, I read from Beckett, the "I can't go on, I'll go on" passage from *The Unnamable*. A few sentences in, I started to feel ridiculous. Why didn't I speak from the heart? Why would I have chosen something that ended *I'll go on*?

John's daughter, who had flown in from overseas, spoke last. She said she never really saw him and didn't really know him, but it was nice to meet all his friends. I wondered what she made of all this, of us, a mishmash of artists, musicians, writers, cooks, and cab drivers that formed her father's social safety net. And it ran both ways. He was the linchpin, the hub, the fastener that made our relationships make sense. Without him, we were just a bunch of people standing around, holding tiny jewelled glasses of mint tea.

After John died, I took a copy of *Godot* I found when we cleaned out his apartment. It had a handwritten prop list and notes in it, and some of Estragon's lines were underscored. At the end, Estragon says, "Yes, let's go." But they don't move.

A few months later, on Christmas, we were all served eviction notices. We fought the landlords, whose company had no name, only a series of numbers, and whose office turned out to be an empty storefront. We fought them, and then eventually we couldn't fight them anymore, and then we left.

Cinema V
Heather O'Neill

When I was eleven, my father was given an envelope of free tickets to Cinema V, the repertory cinema a couple of blocks away from where we lived, in Notre-Dame-de-Grâce. There were Egyptian figures carved into the relief of the building and two columns with the heads of pharaohs on top. In 1984, this was where cool kids hung out. They would swarm around the front of the building, laughing and smoking cigarettes and trying to throw one another into traffic.

The guys dressed in second-hand suits over Talking Heads T-shirts and Converse sneakers. The girls wore heavy black cat eyeliner as though they were members of Andy Warhol's factory. I preferred their outfits to the preppy *St. Elmo's Fire* aesthetic that was mainstream at the time. Those young people went to the mainstream theatre to watch Tom Cruise and Kevin Costner and Meg Ryan be American.

There were two theatres in Cinema V: the Red Room and the Blue Room. The Red Room was more traditional. It had plush velvet chairs and a heavy red curtain that opened up before the film started. This was where they played newer releases, the ones that were too controversial or art house to have runs in regular theatres.

The Blue Room was where I found myself on my first visit and most other days I went. It was a larger theatre but much more rundown. It looked like a rough draft of a cinema. The carpets were dirty and threadbare. The seats were leather with wooden backs, often broken and mostly light blue. There was a filthy barren stage in front of the screen.

In the middle of *Repo Man*, the first film I saw there, a member of the audience climbed up on the stage and began acting out the motions of a character. No one seemed to think it was odd. During a scene where the main character drops his pants, the entire audience screamed at once, "Give him a blow job!" I was startled and had no idea what was going on, but I survived the film and loved it.

After that, I kept going back. You could tell from the way the crowd was dressed whether there was a cult classic playing that night. The stage was often an invitation for someone to run up and begin acting out a scene from the movie. They would be shot like the character and find themselves writhing on the floor. Or they would laugh maniacally like the psychopath above. I found it terrifying at first, but I grew to love this breaking of the fourth wall.

Even when I ran out of free tickets, I kept returning. I'd seen teenagers sneak into the cinema by climbing up the fire escape on the side of the building and entering through an emergency exit near the roof. But I kept paying the child's fare—ninety-nine cents if you were eleven and under—until I was fourteen, five feet ten, and looked older than my age. The people who worked there were always so laid back, they never said anything about it.

I had a wild education in films at Cinema V. By the time I was thirteen, I'd seen virtually every Nouveau Vague film, every Italian realist masterpiece, and all the American classics from the 1970s. I learned about eccentric dialogue. I learned about profundity and horror and abjection. I learned about the sublime and unspeakable. I learned about auteur cinema and distinctive voice. The theatre taught me to look for art outside of the mainstream and how to appreciate works no one else around me could stand.

When I learned that Cinema V was closing, I joined a group of teenagers protesting outside of the theatre. It didn't work, of course. For a brief time, it became a regular movie theatre, and then, after a fire, the building lay deteriorating for decades. There were several attempts to resurrect the space and turn it into a community hub or arts centre. It never surprised me when the plans came to naught, and the building was finally condemned.

The magic of Cinema V was created out of a benevolent neglect, a group of talented programmers, and a mob of curious young adults looking for knowledge about subcultures and punk sensibilities and DIY aesthetics. No logical or political planning could ever recreate that. Now the building stands empty, filled with the ghosts of rebellious teenagers. The pharaohs look ahead, not reporting their crimes.

A Little Bit More Fabulous
Cason Sharpe

For a brief period when I was a student, I worked in the warehouse of a mid-tier luxury clothing brand. I rode the 55 North along Saint-Laurent to Montreal's Garment District four days a week to count dusty boxes of shoes, each pair worth more than my bi-weekly paycheque. After each shift, I rode the 55 South to go to class.

The warehouse operated like a small village. Villagers included the shipping department, which sent product to flagship, outlet, and retail locations across the country; quality control, which assessed product for damage sustained in storage, in transit, or during production; and the e-commerce division, which collected and sent product to individual consumers. Each package was accompanied by a rectangular placard that read, in curly faux-cursive, *Congratulations! Your life is about to get a little bit more fabulous.*

In addition to these departments, whose purposes I more-or-less understood, the warehouse contained a seemingly infinite number of opaque sub-departments created through the bureaucratic mitosis of national logistics. Spatially, these departments could be broken down along racial lines. Downstairs, where manual labour happened—moving, lifting, stacking, unwrapping, sewing, steaming, counting, and folding—was the domain of nonwhite employees, predominately Black or Filipino. The majority of white employees worked behind computers upstairs. The position for which I'd been hired was somewhere between an upstairs job and a downstairs job. My official title was inventory clerk.

The inventory department consisted of me and Katie, a small bubbly woman in her early forties who lived in Laval with her preteen son and yappy Maltese. At the beginning of every shift, we were assigned a section of the warehouse. It was our job to count every product in our assigned section to ensure the accuracy of the company's digital inventory. At the end of every shift, we were to report any discrepancies to our managers upstairs, who would then launch an internal investigation to determine if the day's discrepancies were the result of misallocation, systems error, or shrinkage. In other words, Katie and I were the village narcs.

Katie used to work with the other Filipino

women in quality control, but she had transferred departments a few weeks before I arrived. Some said the transfer was a promotion, earning Katie the disdain of her colleagues along with a modest raise. Others claimed the transfer was a lateral move implemented by management after Katie lodged a complaint against Julie, her long-time coworker and former best friend. Whatever the reason, Katie received an onslaught of whispers, snickers, and stink eyes whenever she walked past quality control, an antagonism only compounded by her new position as warehouse snitch.

Katie and I ate lunch alone, ostracized from the rest of the village. We shouldered a lot of animosity for two superfluous employees with minimum-wage salaries. The company had a litany of safeguards in place to protect against employee theft, including sophisticated surveillance and alarm systems, hard and soft security tags, and mandatory bag checks any time you left the building. Inventory discrepancies were rare and most frequently caused by computer glitches or input mistakes. Only once during my four-month tenure did I come across an item totally unaccounted for: a pair of stilettos gone without a trace. The managers upstairs determined the shoes had likely been stolen, but their investigation yielded no culprit.

How did the warehouse thief do it? How did they evade the security cameras, the alarm systems, the soft tags, the bag checks, me and Katie, and finally, the managers upstairs? Years later, I find myself both impressed and jealous. I never stole a single thing from that job even though my role as inventory clerk put me in the ideal position to cover my tracks. I didn't restrain my sticky fingers out of some moral compunction. Why buy shoes from a company that won't even pay you enough to afford them? I restrained myself because I was scared. I needed the job to pay rent, and what if I got caught?

For their cunning and bravery, the warehouse thief will always have my admiration. I like to picture them, whoever they are, standing on the corner of Saint-Laurent and Chabanel Ouest, waiting for the 55 South, a pair of stilettos on their feet and a rectangular placard tucked into their pocket. I hope their life today is as fabulous as promised.

Once I started seeing the evidence, I couldn't unsee it. First it was the droppings. I started sweeping shit out corners, from underneath our storage island. I even found some in a large mixing bowl. I stopped cooking. I began living off of takeaway chicken from Romados and trusting only food kept in the safety of the fridge. The piles of poison multiplied.

I was under siege. Every time I entered a room or searched through my closet, I expected the worst. I began examining the cracks in the mortar of those perfect brick walls. I'd read that mice can slip through a gap the size of a dime. I kept replacing the poison, but it felt Sisyphean. I gave up on eradication and prayed for things to just not get any worse. This is just what $595 gets you. Cheap apartments are cheap for a reason. I would learn to live with it.

And live with it I did, until one night, maybe a year later. It was still dark, it must have been two or three, and I'd woken up thirsty. I walked into the kitchen, grabbed a glass, and shuffled over to the sink. Then, in the yellow glare of the streetlight, I saw it. A little shadow moving near one of the poison piles. The creature must have heard me, because it bolted—and ran straight into my foot.

Years later, I can still feel that light little thud. We both stood there, no idea what to do next. I saw the mouse, and in it, I saw all the other mice who lived in this home, the unknown dozens who must be hidden all around me now. What did the mouse see in me? The god who brings the pellets? Did it connect me to the deaths of its parents, its siblings, its lovers? Did it see me as the source of those terrible green gifts now working away inside it, causing its body to slowly bleed out internally? Did it wonder why?

The spell broke; the mouse ran off. I stood there for a little bit longer, now fully awake. I knew I wouldn't fall back asleep. I felt unnerved. The worst had happened, and I was still here. I felt bad—after all, it was just a little mouse. I briefly wondered if I should go back to being a vegetarian. But, deep down, I knew I was kidding myself. I still wanted it to die. It was then that I realized, cheap rent or not, it was time to move.

Concrete Dreams
Daniel Allen Cox

Several years ago, I was standing at the corner of Boulevards René-Lévesque and Robert-Bourassa, waiting at a red light to cross. I looked down, saw a copy of *L'Almanach Moderne 1976* lying on the sidewalk, and picked it up. It's not every day you find a time capsule from the year of your birth.

The volume, 700 yellowing pages of perfectly useless marginalia, appears to have been published in late 1975. Before the internet, there was no other single source where you could learn what Quebec strongman Horace Barré ate (up to twelve kilos of meat per sitting), the projected global population in 2150 (256 billion), and the first words spoken on the moon (*Lève, maintenant tu peux y aller*). Most of these things can't be right. The almanac is a palimpsest of errors.

But what fascinates me most are the photos of iron girders and empty shells—the Olympic Stadium and velodrome months behind schedule—juxtaposed against drawings of what they were supposed to look like. The stadium: an oblong dome with a white roof, dimpled like a golf ball, suspended by cables attached to an inclined tower, the Pisa of the supposed New World. The velodrome: more of a potato bug, but equally majestic. There was no way these buildings would be completed on time. *L'Almanach* was asking us to believe in the impossible and to situate ourselves within it.

I cannot separate the Olympic Stadium's history from my own. It's where, at age two, I got my first scar after nose-diving from a folding chair at a religious convention. Other childhood injuries seemed to coincide with the thousands of tears the stadium's two roofs would eventually sustain. Every time a hunk of concrete fell, I broke a finger, a femur, an idea of myself. Le stade is where, beneath the unfinished tower, I saw future Expos Hall of Famers chase down fly balls; it's where I saw my own name lit up on the scoreboard on a school trip. I got my COVID-19 vaccines in the service corridors behind home plate. My family appears to be implicated as well: a friend of my grandfather's apparently stole seven jackhammers from the Olympic construction site and buried them in a front yard in the east end, presumably to later dig up and sell, which he never did. Now

I know why it took the city thirty years to pay off the debt.

L'Almanach refers to the stadium as having l'impression d'intimité, which I can guarantee no one has ever felt. I saw Pink Floyd perform there in 1994, which was just a poor stand-in for their 1977 show in the same centre field, when they thought up the concept behind *The Wall*, a metaphor for separation between audience and stage. This imagined partition is what allowed me to inhabit the stadium at different ages all at once: I waved to myself sitting behind third base from far away in the bleachers, and I watched myself lurk near the home-team dugout while standing in line for a giant pretzel. Maybe this is what the Olympic Park's website means by "a masterpiece of architecture and engineering." It can't be referring to the structure itself.

When I fret that I've chosen a dinosaur of retrofuturism as my favourite Montreal landmark, I remind myself that I voted multiple times against mayoral candidate Denis Coderre, whose grandiose visions of the city included building a new ballpark, another potential dinosaur. But was that because I rejected the hubris of the fever dream—the metaphor cast in concrete—or because I feared the destruction of the old stadium and, with it, my own implied demise? After all, by that point, my bones had become fused with the rebar.

What I omitted about that moment on the street corner was that there were dozens of almanacs of different years at my feet. Who had left them there? What warnings did the other books offer? I was interested only in 1976, but if I had read subsequent editions, I might have found clues on how Montreal can shed nostalgia and embrace futurism for what it is: an alloy of promise and uncertainty.

If anyone is alive in 2150 and they happen to unearth the stadium, I doubt there will be any documentation around to adequately explain the ruins to them. Perhaps the biggest surprise will be seven jackhammers surfacing near the historic site once known as the east end, machines that I'm sure have been tunnelling new visions of the city since the day they were buried.

A Revolution
Tara McGowan-Ross

It wasn't until the bus driver yelled "Terminus!" that I realized I'd missed my stop. As the driver's tone grew impatient, I hauled my luggage onto the corner of Berri and Sainte-Catherine. At twenty years old, I was planting my boots on Montreal soil as a resident of the city for the first time.

I saw the riot cop as the bus pulled away. A paddy wagon had veered around the corner, and out he stepped, wearing full gear less a helmet. He adjusted the armour covering his shins. He had what I would come to understand as Montreal riot-cop posture: ramrod-straight, dominating, but with an eerie hint of dancer grace. His face was young, almost pretty. Then he slipped his helmet on, and he disappeared into a cocoon of anonymous black Kevlar.

It was 2012, and Montrealers were marching up and down the streets with the red square over their hearts. What had begun as a student demonstration against a tuition hike was threatening to bloom into a massive general strike against the Quebec government's austerity politics. As the mid-July sun dipped ominously toward dusk, I knew another night demonstration was set to begin at any moment. It was why I had moved to Montreal in the first place: I was a bored baby radical, looking for the struggle. But not tonight. I had an apartment to find.

I had seven weeks before the protests ended. It was plenty of time. I got distracted, though. I was busy setting up my apartment, gigging for grocery money, wandering the streets at night with open bottles, slack-jawed at the beauty of my new home. The student protests dissipated before I went back to school. I missed the revolution.

Two and a half years later, I finally emerged onto Berri and Sainte-Catherine as a student demonstrator. Our strike didn't last as long in 2015, but it was mine. The 2012 protests had been mythic—inspirational yet far away. This time, it was personal. We were dominating the road, clogging every urban artery, our bodies forcing the drab buildings around us to come alive. Riot cops weaved through us like determined little insects. We didn't care. I was surrounded by thousands of my closest friends. *Whose streets?* we asked. *Our streets*, we answered.

"Eroticism is not sex per se, but the qualities

of vitality, curiosity, and spontaneity that make us feel alive," writes Esther Perel. Sexuality is a manifestation of eroticism but not its only one. Activism can be erotic. So can art, laughter, and platonic conections. Eroticism is what makes the world new. It is the opposite of being dead.

That year, I was head over heels. On picket lines and in strategy meetings, I ached with political desire. I took up smoking, either to feed or to soothe my racing thoughts, I couldn't tell. I couldn't sleep or eat. I was lovesick for revolution. When we talked about the neoliberal politics of austerity, I knew what I meant. I believed in the leftist ideology I espoused: education is a social good.

It was hard to distinguish my political motivations from my personal ones. I was in love with my friends and with one man in particular. The organizing we were doing was a manifestation of our love: we made our love material and then shared it. This made our politics intoxicating when they were going well. It made every failure fundamentally devastating. The failures would arrive soon but not yet. Failure couldn't touch me at Berri and Sainte-Catherine.

I'd been doing too much yelling and marching and too little sleeping and eating. I was planning on meeting a friend of mine for Tex-Mex downtown and then going home to pass out. I saw that man I loved walking down the street. He explained the situation: a class had broken through the picket line on campus and we needed to go make noise and disrupt it. Now. "Are you coming?" he asked. Inside the restaurant, my friend was already ordering lunch. I didn't have any fight left in me. "No," I said.

He went back to the picket line. I got a burrito, went home, and took a nap. Within days, our student movement died out completely. Everyone demonstrating that afternoon spent the next six months in tribunals being threatened with expulsion. I graduated with great distinction and a clean disciplinary record. Space has memory. It tastes like barbacoa and failure at Mackay and De Maisonneuve.

The Pickle Helper
Selena Ross

Passing by Simcha's shop, you wanted to hurry and avert your eyes. The old-school sign was cute, but the fruit piled on a table outdoors, at the corner of Saint-Laurent and Napoleon, sometimes had visible rotten spots. Simcha, a stooped man in a dirty white grocer's coat, would look on as you passed, your bags loaded with food bought elsewhere.

I'd never been inside, but one day, my friend Adam and I were trying to make matzo-ball soup. I had never made it and was, relatedly, not very secure in my Jewishness. We were all jokes, but underneath, I was embarrassingly earnest. Could I do it?

We needed matzo meal and walked into Simcha's gloom, asking about it. He scowled. "There's matzo," he said, pointing to boxes on the shelf. He told us to crush it with a wine bottle like he did as a kid. Matzo meal, or pre-ground matzo, had been common for decades. Adam and I stared, and if Simcha could have spat at us, he would have. We

197

meekly bought a box, went home, washed a wine bottle, and crushed it—the matzo and the soup.

A few months earlier, I told my grandfather that I'd gotten my first-ever apartment, on Rue Clark. I was nineteen and at McGill. It turned out that he'd lived across the street after he'd arrived from Poland at seventeen, in 1929—I could see his old place from my roommate's bedroom.

In the neighbourhood, sixty years felt like barely a blip. The big Warshaw's store had recently disappeared, but L. Berson & Fils was still engraving Hebrew tombstones near the tiny synagogue across from my sister's apartment. Businessmen streamed into Moishe's and students wandered into Slovenia deli. Most of Montreal's Jews had moved to the suburbs, but their old haunts lived on.

A while after the matzo episode, I noticed a sign on the door of Simcha's shop: "Wanted: pickle helper." Simcha was, as always, alone inside. My sister and I wondered how he survived, and I'd occasionally bought an apple from him out of pity. "I saw your ad for a pickle helper," I said. He glowered and looked me over. "I usually get a boy for that," he said. Picturing a knickerbocker-wearing lad from the musical *Newsies*, I shrugged apologetically. "I think I can do it," I said. "What exactly is the job?"

Simcha led me back to his tiny storeroom. The produce in front may have been slowly rotting, but back here, Simcha was a cucumber artist; he lifted the tops off huge barrels, revealing a murky, scummy liquid. I'd never even considered the idea that dill pickles could be homemade. *I'm going to do it*, I thought, suddenly passionate about learning the trade.

"Come every morning at 6 a.m. and stir the pickles," he said. Then I'd come back around 4 p.m. and stir them again. There may have been other tasks—I can't remember. I recall him saying the job paid about $3 an hour, less than half of minimum wage, and I already had a summer job. "So I'd need to be here twice a day at a strict time, and you'd give me about $5 a day?" I asked, trying to keep my voice polite. Yes, he said. I told him I just couldn't manage it and that I was really sorry.

In 2022, Slovenia announced that it was packing up, its red-and-yellow sign about to disappear forever. When L. Berson & Fils had moved off the Main, a few years earlier, I'd teared up. When Moishe's left, in 2021, I covered it as a reporter, feeling pandemic grim. But, now, I thought of Simcha.

I recently learned that Montreal filmmaker Ezra Soiferman made a documentary about Simcha, specifically about how his legendary pickle recipe died with him in 2005. He was born in Romania, worked on a ship, survived the Holocaust, and had that shop with his wife for forty years. They never had kids.

I didn't need to know about the lost recipe to regret not apprenticing myself to Simcha. My grandfather, my zaida, died the year I moved to Clark. I never met my grandmother, only to realize in my thirties that no one in my family even knew where she was born. The hundreds of letters she wrote in Yiddish were thrown out long ago by some relative who, I imagine, felt there were countless ones like them—which there were, back then.

These days, my nostalgia for the old Montreal can be overpowering; it sometimes feels like COVID-19 is erasing people and places right before my eyes, stopping the generations from their mingling. But, really, I think the virus just made me finally face it.

Simcha, of all people, wouldn't care. He would tell me to make my own pickles or just shut up.

Up on the Roof
H Felix Chau Bradley

"Wait there," I say over my shoulder to my date, whose face blurs in the purple light of early sunrise. "I've done this a million times."

It's not true—I've watched someone else do it—but I feign confidence. I hoist myself on top of the recycling bin, armpits slick with summer sweat, and yank the rusted metal of the fire escape ladder, meant to be tucked out of reach, so that its first step meets the garbage-puddled concrete of the alley. I jump back onto the ground and place a foot on the metal slats. "Come on," I say with what I hope is a rakish grin. "The trick is not to look down."

My date follows me hesitantly up the swaying five-storey stairway. Once we reach the top, uncertainty turns to elation. "This is incredible," they say, surveying the extensive, multilevel rooftop. I lead them past filmy skylights and ventilation units until we are at the edge, looking down over the balustrades of the Rialto Theatre. Avenue du Parc is laid out below us, the mountain hulking darkly beyond. We share our takeout poutine from Nouveau Palais, which is still an all-night diner, and succumb to the romance of a rooftop sunrise.

The Rialto Theatre is one of the most recognizable buildings in the Mile End. It presides over the corner of Parc and Bernard, often boasting a long lineup beneath its marquis. Constructed in 1924 and designated a National Historic Site in 1993 due to its ornate Paris Opera–inspired facade and its baroque interior, it reopened as a multipurpose, multiroom venue in 2010.

In the summers of the early 2010s, the Rialto rooftop becomes my go-to spot for dates. I like the intimacy of letting a new crush in on a city secret. In these years, everyone is always screening films in back alleys, playing shows in underpasses and abandoned tunnels, partying on rooftops and in vacant warehouses, climbing into concrete ruins armed with bike lights and curiosity. For a certain population of students and artists and activist-workers, rent is cheap and working hours are flexible. Staying up all night to ramble is the norm.

One night, after a party or an after-party, a big group of us gets bold and clambers up to the roof together to keep hanging out. That's the clincher: the cops show up and escort us down, threatening large tickets. The secret doesn't feel like a secret anymore, and I soon stop visiting.

Years later, I am working for Pop Montreal, the Mile End music-and-arts festival. For some years, Pop has set up its festival headquarters in the Rialto complex, using its labyrinthine rooms and theatres as venues and galleries, including the rooftop, which is one of the festival's most coveted spots for artists to play.

The Mile End has changed noticeably. For Rent signs are cropping up everywhere. Small businesses are disappearing. Much community ire is directed at Shiller Lavy, a real estate company that is buying up the neighbourhood's buildings and slapping renters with massive hikes. When COVID-19 hits, in 2020, landlords have the option to claim government subsidies that allow them to reduce or suspend rent, but many don't bother. If the Mile End felt gutted before, now it is dangerously close to a ghost town.

Pop staunchly holds its annual festival that fall—a hybrid version, with most shows streaming online and a few select live performances, mainly in small outdoor venues. Naturally, the Rialto rooftop is one of the live stages. On the last night of what has been a somewhat strange, subdued edition of the festival, the staff assembles on the Rialto roof. Someone DJs from their phone through the speaker system, and suddenly the energy is back. I'm not trying to seduce anyone now—my partner has long gone to bed, leaving me to stay up with the Pop crew. But I get a surge of that old ecstasy, up here on the roof, dancing with friends I haven't been able to see in months.

Looking over the vertiginous parapet, I can almost imagine that nothing has changed down below, that rent is affordable, that the shops are bustling, that Big Tech hasn't moved in to stay, that the pandemic isn't wreaking its lasting devastation. But nostalgia can be simplistic and misleading, so I turn away, back to my friends and coworkers, who are lit up with joy.

The Balcony
Derek Webster

The balcony was small and semicircular, and you could barely squeeze a chair onto it. Jutting out from the corner of the building at Clark and Prince Arthur, it was more ornamental than functional, a pretty thing to admire from the street. Negotiating its small dimensions was something of an acquired art: one had to swing the ancient wooden exterior door half open, step around, then close it again before sitting. The exterior door never fully closed either—a drafty fact my roommate Dunc cursed throughout the winter. The railing was so low that leaning back in the chair felt like toying with death. For both of us to fit, one person had to take to the cold balcony floor, so we usually brought out the bath mat to sit on.

After the school year ended, in late April—Dunc and I were arts students at McGill—we stayed on to take a summer course or two. Summer courses were fun. Students and teachers were in good moods, less stressed, more willing to discuss ideas during and after class—and Montreal in late May and June was perfect barbecue weather.

The balcony was just big enough for our prized hibachi.

Chicken, sausages, burgers—Dunc always did them right. He knew how to achieve the good life quickly: a baguette, goat cheese and olives from La Vieille Europe, a Burgundy or Chablis from the SAQ. Or, in winter, after a trip to Warshaw or Les 4 Freres, a chicken to roast alongside garlic, onions, carrots, and potatoes. If our laughing-wild friend Brigitte visited from Toronto, her legendary meat sauce would definitely soon follow.

Dunc was a good roommate, and talking with him was never boring. In warm weather, he and I sat out on the balcony and read together. While I memorized Malvolio's lines about cross-gartered yellow stockings, Dunc would smoke between sessions of *Moby Dick* or gather his thoughts on the use of irony by Margaret Atwood. I have a picture of him from those days: midmorning on the balcony in his white hotel bathrobe, hair everywhere, looking groggy, about to light up a cigarette. It's not a flattering picture. But it reminds me of the bleary nonchalance of those days and why I liked them.

Because our balcony was on the second floor, we could be recognized by people coming down

Prince Arthur from the university, and we had a partial view of the action on Saint-Laurent. People dropped by to say hi at random hours, often after getting tipsy on the Main—smiling, flush-faced people you'd met in a class or some activities club, who you'd talked to maybe twice. One made fast friends back then. Getting to know people felt like an adventure.

Those balcony days were the freest I've ever felt: a head full of new ideas, a glass of beer or wine in hand, the evening's hours stretching out ahead—and my main purpose: to talk, listen, and savour the simple joy of being present in the moment.

When middle age feels like a series of disappointments waiting to present themselves—a state of mind we call *jaded*—I try to remember that an ideal mix of innocence and experience still exists and that lessons learned in my twenties can be relearned at any age: Don't lean back too far. Keep looking out at the world. Freedom means time. The good life is within reach.

That's how I felt on that little balcony.

CONTRIBUTORS

Nour Abi-Nakhoul is a Montreal-based writer whose work has appeared in *The Cut, Xtra, Chatelaine,* and elsewhere.

Fionn Adamian is a master's student in European literatures at Humboldt-Universität zu Berlin.

Correy Baldwin is a copy editor and writer living in Montreal, working with *Uppercase* magazine and McGill-Queen's University Press.

Hélène Bauer is a Swiss-French journalist who spent 10 years of her life in Montreal. She now lives in Paris, where she is editor-in-chief for the digital publication of the travel magazine *EnVols*.

andrea bennett is the managing editor of *The Tyee* and the former editor-in-chief of *Maisonneuve*. Their most recent book is *Like a Boy but Not a Boy*, an essay collection.

Melissa Bull is a writer and translator. She lives in Montreal.

Kyle Carney is a writer, runner, and birdwatcher. He lives in Lachine, Quebec.

H Felix Chau Bradley is the author of *Personal Attention Roleplay*, which was a finalist for the Danuta Gleed Literary Award and the Kobo Rakuten Emerging Writer Prize, as well as the poetry chapbook *Automatic Object Lessons*. They are the fiction editor for *This Magazine*, an acquiring editor for Metonymy Press, and the host of *Strange Futures*, a speculative fiction book club. They live in Tiohtià:ke (Montreal).

Eva Crocker is a writer and PhD student at Concordia University, where she is researching visual art in Newfoundland and Labrador. Her short story collection *Barrelling Forward* won the Alistair MacLeod Award for Short Fiction and the CAA Emerging Author's Award. Her debut novel, *All I Ask*, was longlisted for the 2020 Giller Prize and won the BMO Winterset Award.

Haley Cullingham is a book-and-magazine editor from Toronto. She currently works at Penguin Random House Canada, editing work for *Hazlitt*, Strange Light Books, and McClelland & Stewart.

Crystal Chan is a writer, editor, and producer. Originally from Hong Kong, she is based in Tiohtià:ke (Montreal), where she serves as an executive board member of the Quebec Writers' Federation. She is a professor in the creative writing department of the University of British Columbia and an editor at UBC Press for RavenSpace publishing.

Daniel Allen Cox's essays have appeared in *Maisonneuve*, *Electric Literature*, *Literary Hub*, *The Malahat Review*, and elsewhere. His work has been nominated for a National Magazine Award and named notable in Best American Essays. He is the author of four novels and a memoir-in-essays forthcoming from Penguin Random House Canada.

Michelle Deines writes in multiple genres including drama and nonfiction. Her works have appeared onstage in Calgary and Vancouver and in the pages of various magazines across Canada. She is a faculty member of the theatre department at Capilano University, where she teaches theatre history and playwriting. She lives in Vancouver.

Megan Dolski has worked as a reporter for the *Globe and Mail*, the *Toronto Star*, CTV News and the Canadian Press. She was a fact-checker at *Maisonneuve* before she left Montreal the time before last time. These days, she lives and works in Paris.

Eli Tareq El Bechelany-Lynch is a queer Arab poet living in Tiohtià:ke, unceded Kanien'kehá:ka territory. They were longlisted for the CBC poetry prize in 2019. Their first book, *knot body*, was published by Metatron Press in 2020. Their second book, *The Good Arabs*, was published by Metonymy Press in 2021.

Jason Freure is the author of *Everyone Rides the Bus in a City of Losers* (ECW) and the former publisher of *The Puritan*. His writing has appeared in *Canadian Notes and Queries*, *Spacing*, the *Montreal Review of Books*, *carte blanche*, and others.

Ziya Jones is a senior editor at *Xtra*. Their writing has appeared in *Chatelaine*, *Eater*, and the *Toronto Star*, among other places.

Maija Kappler is a writer and editor from Montreal who now lives in Toronto. She has worked at the Canadian Press and *HuffPost Canada*, was the recipient of a Canadian Online Publishing Award, and has had her writing published in *The Walrus*, the *Globe and Mail*, *La Presse*, and *Chatelaine*.

Will Keats-Osborn is a writer and sociologist living on BC's Sunshine Coast.

Erica Ruth Kelly is a Montreal-born, Toronto-dwelling writer, storyteller, and speaker. Her work has appeared in the *Montreal Gazette*, the *Globe and Mail*, *Buzzfeed*, and *Maisonneuve*, among others. A mental health advocate and nonprofit worker, she sings in Toronto's largest 2SLGTBQQIA+ choir.

Mim Kempson is an Australian public speaker, narrative therapist, and relationship coach working mainly with 2SLGTBQQIA+ individuals and couples.

Katherine Laidlaw is a feature writer and essayist based in Toronto. Her stories have appeared in *Wired*, *Outside*, *The Atlantic*, *Marie Claire*, *Toronto Life*, and *The Walrus*.

Chandler Levack is a writer, journalist, and filmmaker from Toronto. Her writing has been featured in publications including the *Globe and Mail*, *Rolling Stone*, *Toronto Life*, and *Maisonneuve*. Her short films and music videos have screened at the Toronto International Film Festival, the sxsw Film Festival, and the Museum of Modern Art.

Anna Leventhal is the author of the short story collection *Sweet Affliction* (Invisible Publishing). Her writing has appeared in *Geist*, *Maisonneuve*, *The Puritan*, *carte blanche*, *Lettres québécoises*, and elsewhere. After twenty-odd years in Tiohtià:ke (Montreal), she now lives in Winnipeg, Treaty 1 territory.

Rosie Long Decter is a writer and musician based in Montreal. Her work has appeared in *This Magazine*, *The New Quarterly*, *Xtra*, *Herizons*, and elsewhere. She performs regularly with her band Bodywash and sings backup in a Fleetwood Mac cover band.

Alex Manley is a Montreal-based writer, editor, and poet. They are the translator of *Made-Up: A True Story of Beauty Culture under Late Capitalism* (Coach House Books).

Tara McGowan-Ross is an urban Mi'kmaw multidisciplinary artist. She is the author of the poetry collections *Girth* and *Scorpion Season* and the memoir *Nothing Will Be Different*. She lives in Montreal, where she is a theatre critic, a Substack columnist, and the host of Librairie Drawn & Quarterly's Indigenous Literatures book club.

Jeff Miller is the author of *Ghost Pine: All Stories True*. He lived in Montreal from 1999 to 2017 and now calls Nova Scotia home.

Sara Black McCulloch is a Montreal-born writer living in Toronto. Her work has appeared in *Hazlitt*, *The Believer*, and the *Los Angeles Review of Books*, among others.

Sean Michaels is a novelist, short story writer, and critic. His awards include the Scotiabank Giller Prize, the QWF Paragraphe Hugh MacLennan Prize for Fiction, the Grand Prix Numix, the Prix Gémeaux, and two National Magazine Awards. He lives in Montreal, where he founded the music blog *Said the Gramophone*.

Heather O'Neill is an award-winning novelist, short story writer, and essayist. Her works include *Lullabies for Little Criminals*, *The Lonely Hearts Hotel*, and *When We Lost Our Heads*. She lives in Montreal.

Deborah Ostrovsky is a writer, editor, and translator living in Montreal. Her nonfiction has appeared in magazines and journals in the US and Canada, including *Tablet*, *Geist*, and *Maisonneuve*, and her satire has been published in *McSweeney's Internet Tendency* and *Points in Case*.

André Picard is the health columnist at the *Globe and Mail* and the author of the bestselling book *Neglected No More*.

Sejla Rizvic is a writer and fact checker living in New York and a former editorial fellow at *The Walrus*. Her work has appeared in American and Canadian publications including the *New York Times*, *The Cut*, *The Tyee*, and *The Walrus*.

Selena Ross was the editor-in-chief of Maisonneuve from 2018 to 2020. She's also a long-time reporter who has worked for the *Globe and Mail*, the *Washington Post*, the *Halifax Chronicle Herald*, and CTV Montreal. Originally from Ottawa, she adopted Montreal as her home city in 2003.

Bernard Rudny is a strategic communications consultant who works with nonprofits.

Katie Sehl is a writer and editor based in Montreal. Her writing and photography have appeared in *en-*

Route, *Fortune*, *Maisonneuve*, *Vice*, and other publications.

Cason Sharpe is a writer currently based in Toronto. His first collection of stories, *Our Lady of Perpetual Realness*, was published by Metatron Press in 2017.

Valerie Silva is a Montreal-based writer and editor who currently heads *Eater Montreal*. Her work has been published in *enRoute*, *Maisonneuve*, *Elle Canada*, and elsewhere.

Lindsay Tapscott is a film producer, writer, and editor living in Toronto.

Carly Rosalie Vandergriendt's writing has appeared in *Journey Prize Stories 30*, *The Malahat Review*, *The Fiddlehead*, *Room*, and other publications. She lives and works in Tiohtià:ke (Montreal).

Daniel Viola is the senior editor at *The Walrus* and a former editor-in-chief of *Maisonneuve*. He currently lives in London, UK.

Galadriel Watson is a comics artist and the author of twenty-four children's books. Her writing has also appeared in outlets like the *Globe and Mail*, the *Washington Post*, and *Discover*.

Derek Webster is the founding editor-publisher of *Maisonneuve*. His first book of poems, *Mockingbird*, was a Gerald Lampert Award finalist for best poetry debut in Canada. He lives in Montreal.

Jessica Wei is a writer and editor based in Toronto.

Gleb Wilson is a bookseller currently living in Los Angeles.

ACKNOWLEDGEMENTS

With thanks to all contributing writers for permission to reprint pieces originally published in *Maisonneuve* magazine.

Melissa Bull's "Parc La Fontaine Times Two" appeared in Issue 40 (Summer 2011). Chandler Levack's "La Misérable" appeared in Issue 41 (Fall 2011). Sean Michaels's "The Battle of the Bands" appeared in Issue 43 (Spring 2012). Crystal Chan's "Death in a French Class" appeared in Issue 44 (Summer 2012). Correy Baldwin's "Il Et It Une" appeared in Issue 46 (Winter 2012). Bernard Rudny's "Where the Streets Have Strange Names" appeared in Issue 47 (Spring 2013). Erica Ruth Kelly's "How to Clean a Conspiracy Theorist's Apartment" appeared in Issue 49 (Fall 2013). Katherine Laidlaw's "A Mile End Beginning" appeared in Issue 50 (Winter 2013). Sejla Rizvic's "The Spirit and the Flesh" appeared in Issue 51 (Spring 2014). Gleb Wilson's "The Ghost in the Machine" appeared in Issue 52 (Summer 2014). Lindsay Tapscott's "The City Undressed" appeared in Issue 53 (Fall 2014). Haley Cullingham's "Old Haunts" appeared in Issue 54 (Winter 2014). Jessica Wei's "Under the Paifang" appeared in Issue 55 (Spring 2015). Sara Black McCulloch's "Catching the Light" appeared in Issue 56 (Summer 2015). Deborah Ostrovsky's "Les Enfants du Roi" appeared in Issue

57 (Fall 2015). Mim Kempson's "As the Snow Flies" appeared in Issue 58 (Winter 2015). Megan Dolski's "Remembrance of Poutines Past" appeared in Issue 59 (Spring 2016). Jason Freure's "Cat People" appeared in Issue 60 (Summer 2016). Deborah Ostrovsky's "No Woman Is an Island" appeared in Issue 61 (Fall 2016). Hélène Bauer's "A Site for Soirées" appeared in Issue 62 (Winter 2016). Maija Kappler's "The Still Waters of the Saint Lawrence" appeared in Issue 63 (Spring 2017). Kyle Carney's "Ollies in Outremont" appeared in Issue 64 (Summer 2017). Erica Ruth Kelly's "You Want to Travel with Him" appeared in Issue 65 (Fall 2017). Katie Sehl's "A Schwartz's in Paris" appeared in Issue 66 (Winter 2017). Will Keats-Osborn's "Leaf Thief" appeared in Issue 67 (Spring 2018). Ziya Jones's "On the Lam" appeared in Issue 68 (Summer 2018). Michelle Deines's "Notre Dame D'Espace" appeared in Issue 69 (Fall 2018). Carly Rosalie Vandergriendt's "Home Ice" appeared in Issue 70 (Winter 2018). andrea bennett's "The Rides of March" appeared in Issue 71 (Spring 2019). Fionn Adamian's "Melting Pot" appeared in Issue 72 (Summer 2019). Eva Crocker's "Peak Performance" appeared in Issue 73 (Fall 2019). Deborah Ostrovsky's "Reading the Signs" appeared in Issue 74 (Winter 2019). Jeff Miller's "Melting Away" appeared in Issue 75 (Spring 2020). André Picard's "Highs and Lows" appeared in Issue 76 (Summer 2020). Galadriel Watson's "Out of the Cave" appeared in Issue 77 (Fall 2020). Valerie Silva's "Vanishing Act"

appeared in Issue 78 (Winter 2020). Eli Tareq El Bechelany-Lynch's "Queer Atmosphere" appeared in Issue 79 (Spring 2021). Nour Abi-Nakhoul's "Good Neighbours" appeared in Issue 80 (Summer 2021). Alex Manley's "Past Curfew" appeared in Issue 81 (Fall 2021). Ziya Jones's "The Plaza" appeared in Issue 82 (Winter 2021). Rosie Long Decter's "The Shape of a Scene" appeared in Issue 83 (Spring 2022). H Felix Chau Bradley's "Up on the Roof" appeared in Issue 84 (Summer 2022). Selena Ross's "The Pickle Helper" appeared in Issue 85 (Fall 2022).

LAND ACKNOWLEDGEMENT

We would like to acknowledge and respect that we are publishing from Tiohtià:ke, the Kanien'kéha name for a historic place for gathering and trade for many First Nations. It is unceded traditional Indigenous territory, where the lands and people have a history and legacy that is long and deep, and on which there have now been non-Indigenous settlers for more than 375 years. It has been home to many Indigenous people from across Turtle Island, as are the many traditional territories in which all Canadian publishers work and live. As publishers we know we cannot rewrite our history but we can be part of a concerted effort to contribute to reconciliation between Indigenous Peoples and settlers—we have a special role to play in that process.